P.E. Teacher's Complete Fitness and Skills Development Activities Program

Jeff Carpenter

Parker Publishing
West Nyack, NY 10994

Library of Congress Cataloging-in-Publication Data

Carpenter, Jeff.

    P.E. teacher's complete fitness & skills development activities program / Jeff Carpenter

       p. cm.

    Includes bibliographical references.

    ISBN 0-13-022817-6

    1. Physical education for children.   2. Education, Elementary--Activity programs. I. Title.   II. Title: Physical education teacher's complete fitness and skills development activities program.

GV443.C374   2000

372.86—dc21   99-37792

                                              CIP

Acquisitions Editor: Susan Kolwicz
Production Editor: Mariann Hutlak
Interior Design / Formatting: Dee Coroneos
Composition: Inkwell Publishing Services

Printed in the United States of America

10 9 8 7 6 5 4 3 2 1

ISBN 0-13-022817-6

PARKER PUBLISHING COMPANY
West Nyack, NY 10994

hhtp://www.phdirect.com

Dedicated to Jonathan
and all other children and young adults making
an effort to gain the skills and knowledge
necessary to lead a healthy and active lifestyle.

ACKNOWLEDGMENTS

The author gratefully acknowledges the assistance and support provided by the following professionals for their efforts in compiling this publication: Greg Santora, Lori Pritchett, and Tara Spencer—Olympia Public Schools; Diane Tunnell, Ed.D., Gonzaga University; Alice-Elizabeth Carpenter, Deborah Koss-Warner, and Jonathan Carpenter—illustrators and photography.

FOREWORD

"What am I going to do in physical education today?" What experiences can I bring my students that will have a positive impact on their lives? Every teacher asks these questions over and over. Jeff Carpenter's *P. E. Teacher's Complete Fitness and Skills Development Activities Program* will help you answer those questions. This book will provide you with more than one hundred ideas to incorporate into your program. Students will be challenged with new ways to accomplish physical tasks. They will be creative in their solutions as well as using critical-thinking and decision-making skills with these innovative solutions. Your students will walk away from the gymnasium saying, "Hey, that was fun, and I learned something useful."

The *P. E. Teacher's Complete Fitness and Skills Development Activities Program* is designed for you!!! The activities are easy to incorporate, require minimal set-up time, and are fun. Jeff Carpenter has brought over 27 years of experience as a physical educator, and combined it with his learning experiences and the experiences of colleagues and students to provide a new and exciting resource. As a colleague of Jeff's for over 10 years, I am excited to add this book to my collection.

Motivating students to be physically active is a challenge. Jeff's ideas represent his dedication to enhancing each student's lifestyle by providing activities that are motivating, and relevant, and that allow for active physical involvement. I am certain that, by incorporating this resource into your program, you will find new ideas that make your teaching more enjoyable and the students' experiences more rewarding.

Diane C. Tunnell, Ed.D.
Director, Physical Education
Gonzaga University
Spokane, Washington

ABOUT THE AUTHOR

JEFF CARPENTER, M.S.P.E., has taught and administered elementary, middle, and high school physical education, health, and athletic programs for over 27 years. Prior to becoming the Supervisor of Health and Fitness Education for the Olympia School District in 1994, he served for 10 years as the Washington State Supervisor of Physical Education. Jeff's active presentations at national, state, and regional conferences—including the National AAHPERD Convention and the President's Council on Physical Fitness and Sport Regional Worshops—continually receive excellent reviews. His professional involvement includes terms as president of the Washington Alliance for HPERD and service on numerous regional and national committees, including the National Physical Best Steering Committee, and being named an "AAHPERD National Physical Best Expert." Jeff has received many awards and citations, including the National AAHPERD Honor Award, Washington Physical Educator of the Year, and the Meritorious Service Award.

ABOUT THIS GUIDE

The *P.E. Teacher's Complete Fitness and Skills Development Activities Program* is designed to provide a variety of techniques, activities, and ready-to-use material to implement an effective student-centered physical education program at the intermediate and middle level grades. Each "success-oriented" activity is designed for maximum participation and student success within a variety of instructional settings.

This guide is based on the belief that physical education is an integral part of the total education process that focuses on the intellectual, social, emotional, and physical needs of all students. Provided in the seven sections are over 100 new, exciting skill enhancement and lead-up activities along with interactive "Study Guides" for all activities and concepts presented. Also included are interdisciplinary lessons in math, social studies, history, and health, premade tests of activity-based and health-related knowledge, plus student journals, logs, and worksheets, with age appropriate written knowledge based tests.

Intermediate and middle-level physical educators and classroom teachers have successfully used each activity, journal, student log, or test in a variety of school settings. Using the concepts and activities provided, teachers have found students to be more excited and motivated than when a more traditional approach was utilized. Students know what is expected each day, are provided individual and appropriate challenges, and are constantly moving and having fun.

In *P.E. Teacher's Complete Fitness and Skills Development Activities Program,* activities are presented in an easy-to-follow format. Each activity includes a listing of the focus area along with a brief overview of the total activity. This is followed by a listing of all equipment necessary, grade level suggestions and modifications, "Success Notes" (how to increase motivation, participation, or ability), and a step-by-step description of the procedure and any necessary diagrams of the setting and student movement patterns. Additionally, you'll find a number of reproducible record-keeping aids, surveys, and quizzes—especially in Sections 4 through 7—to help you and your students monitor their progress.

Following is a brief section-by-section overview:

Section 1, *"Organization Through Activity,"* provides concepts and techniques for successfully "turning kids on to activity." You will find ideas to enhance communication between teacher and student, the concepts necessary to develop successful lessons, successful methodologies to make use of student assistants, and meaningful assessments.

Section 2, *"Fitness Development,"* gives you new and exciting activities and concepts to enhance the health-related physical fitness of students. Activities range from the very basic to those involving equipment and making use of previously learned skills.

Section 3, *"Skill Development and Lead-Up Activities,"* provides over 100 activities designed to allow students to learn new skills, enhance previously learned skills, and successfully participate in a variety of individual, team, and cooperative experiences. Included are informational "Study Guides" that provide detailed information on the history, definitions, rules, and basic strategies for each activity.

Section 4, *"Games That Teach,"* offers unique and exciting activities that allow students to enhance their physical skills while making use of math, social studies, health, and science knowledge and skills.

Section 5, *"Healthy Lifestyles,"* presents activities that provide an ideal way to connect theory lessons with practical application situations to assist students in developing personal health, fitness, and activity goals leading to a personal health and fitness lifestyle plan.

Section 6, *"Keeping Track,"* provides two different sets of knowledge-based tests. The first, the "Fit Quiz," assesses the student's knowledge regarding personal fitness development. The second, the "Opinion Poll," allows students to answer questions related to various activities, such as Soccer, Volleyball, Badminton, Golf, and Pickleball. Answer keys are provided for both the "Fit Quiz" and "Opinion Poll" tests. Included in this section are "Skill and Fitness Journals." These interactive journals provide students with an opportunity to record their efforts in class challenges and skill tasks.

Section 7, *"Activity Motivators,"* addresses the issues of goal setting; individualization of learning, including working with special needs populations; and the provision of rewards for student achievement.

In our desire to develop and implement meaningful physical education programs, we must continually look for new ideas and resource material that keep all students actively involved in enjoyable and worthwhile activities. With this quest in mind, the concepts and activities presented in *P.E. Teacher's Complete Fitness and Skills Development Activities Program* have been developed. It is my hope that you not only will make use of these activities but will expand upon them to benefit your students by allowing them to achieve at their highest potential.

Jeff Carpenter

MAKING THE MOST
OF THESE ACTIVITIES

Each activity in this guide is presented in an easy-to-use format that allows for immediate use. You will find

- The lesson focus, which highlights the major objectives and general activities
- A detailed list of all equipment needs for the activity
- Modifications for use with various grade levels
- Ideas to assist in making the activity a success with students
- Step-by-step instructions on how to organize and present the activity

| Fitness Activities | Skill Development | Games That Teach | Healthy Lifestyles | Keeping Track |

ACTIVITY: THE NAME OF THE ACTIVITY

Focus/ Knowledge Skill	Equipment Needed	Suggested Grade Levels
The general goals and objectives of the activity, along with a general overview.	What specific equipment is needed to do the activity.	Grade levels at which the activity has been successfully used and any modifications to accommodate developmental levels.

Success Notes Teaching hints to make the activity a success for all—both students and teachers.

MAKING IT WORK
All you need to know to organize and teach a successful activity.

CONTENTS

SECTION 6
Keeping Track   247

Keeping Track   248

SECTION 7
Activity Motivators 279

SECTION 1

Organization Through Activity

Program Goals

- **P**articipate in developmentally appropriate physical activity to develop and maintain appropriate levels of skill and fitness.

- **F**oster creativity.

- **L**earn healthy and safe practices.

- **E**stablish self-expression and meaningful communication.

- **D**evelop self-understanding and acceptance of others.

Organization Through Activity

✔ **Characteristics of Successful Physical Education Programs**

✔ **Turning Kids On to Physical Activity**
  ➤ Organizing for Success
    ■ In the Locker Room
    ■ When the Locker Room Is Not Used
    ■ Activity and Roll Taking

✔ **Challenge Stations**

✔ **Planning Successful Lessons**
  ➤ Core Activities Unit Plan
  ➤ Preclass Challenges
  ➤ Developmental Fitness Activities
  ➤ Lesson-Core Activities
  ➤ Closing Activities

✔ **Student Assistants**
  ➤ Expectations

✔ **Assessment Made Easy**
  ➤ Video Reviews
  ➤ Peer Observations
  ➤ Participation Observations

✔ **Conclusion**

CHARACTERISTICS OF SUCCESSFUL PHYSICAL EDUCATION PROGRAMS

THE STUDENTS

✔ *All students actively participate in developmentally appropriate activities.*

✔ *All students show enthusiasm about activities.*

✔ *All students work on task to achieve stated goals.*

✔ *All students display respect and consideration for others.*

✔ *All students use equipment and supplies appropriately.*

THE PROGRAM

✔ *There is a planned sequential program of developmentally appropriate knowledge and skill.*

✔ *All students are treated with dignity and respect, regardless of ability.*

✔ *Program expectations are clearly communicated to both students and parents.*

✔ *Individual differences and personal goals are recognized in assessing progress toward programmatic goals.*

✔ *All necessary equipment and supplies are available in an appropriate amount so that all students may be actively engaged in each activity.*

TURNING KIDS ON TO PHYSICAL ACTIVITY

Students tend to like activities and situations in which they are successful. With success comes confidence which acts as a barrier against failure. The greater the number of successful experiences students have, the more willing they are to risk failure in activities not yet mastered. Therefore, in organizing and managing programs providing for numerous successes, opportunities must be a major goal.

The first step in this process is to develop a comprehensive plan. The development of this plan should focus on implementation of a purposeful program with stated, and achievable, goals and carefully planned instruction that leads to the accomplishment of both program and student goals. Organize classes for success. Research tells us that a large block of potential activity time is spent on organization and management tasks. Following are suggestions on how to reduce that time and increase student activity time.

ORGANIZING FOR SUCCESS

Providing for successful experiences begins as students enter the gym or locker room. They want to know what they will be doing and what is expected throughout the period. Posting daily activity signs helps them and assists teachers in their planning process.

IN THE LOCKER ROOM
As students enter the locker room, they should see each teacher's posted color-coded signs indicating where the class will meet, preclass activity challenges, developmental fitness activities, lesson-core activities, and closing activities.

Location Cards:	These cards indicate where the specific classes will meet, what activities they will be doing, and any special announcements or activities taking place.
Preclass Challenges:	Students expect to be active in physical education classes. To meet this need, and to move students quickly from the locker room, provide preclass challenges for extra credit.
Developmental Fitness:	Each class should begin with a focused fitness activity. These activities vary with abilities and class focus. This card should include formations (circuit, lines, etc.), leaders, and the specific activity.
Lesson-Core Activities:	Note the instructional focus of the day, providing information on drills or games to be played.
Closing Activity:	Provide students with an opportunity to play a quick, low-organized game where all can be successful.

WHEN THE LOCKER ROOM IS NOT USED

For classes that do not change clothes for class, posting signs on the entrance to the gym and meeting the class outside for a brief discussion of the day's activities and expectations works well. This format allows students to enter the gym with the necessary information to begin activities immediately.

SAMPLE CARDS

Today Class Will Meet:

Mr. Spencer—Main Gym West Side

Mr. Monroe—Aux. Gym

Before Class Challenge

Mr. Spencer—Rope Skipping and Juggling

Mr. Monroe—Accuracy Toss and Frisbee Toss

Fitness Activity

Mr. Spencer—Student Leader Exercises

Mr. Monroe—Team Prediction

Lesson Core

Mr. Spencer—Volleyball:
Jump and Touch, Partner Wall Volley, "King of the Court"

Mr. Monroe—Pickleball:
Forehand and Backhand Review, Volley Relay, Doubles Play

Special announcements can also be posted in this manner.

ACTIVITY AND ROLL TAKING

Each period, potential activity time is used to take roll. This time can be turned into an activity time that allows for individual student contact, goal setting, and assessment.

Three-Minute Jog After completing the preclass challenge, the signal to "jog" is given and students begin to jog around the gym for 3 minutes. After completing the 3 minutes, students pass the teacher at the center line and tell how many laps they have run. After all laps are recorded, look to see who has not given a score; those students are absent.

While participating in this activity, students can be establishing goals. The first time they run, a baseline is established; each subsequent time the activity is completed, a new score is recorded. Students should be encouraged to beat their previous score by at least a half lap. Respond positively to students as they give their lap count.

Cooperative Warm-Up Arrange seven stations around the sides of the gym. At each station place enough "station cards" for each group of two students. Each "station card" contains a description of the station.

Students, in-groups of two, move through the stations. As they complete one station they take a card and move to the next area. After completing all stations cards are turned in and student names are checked off on the roll sheet.

Sample Stations:

1. Run 1 lap around the gym together with your hands on the waist of your partner.

2. Running with your partner, touch 20 different lines in the gym.

3. Face your partner and sit down and stand up 10 times in a row; keep moving together.

4. Do 15 curl-ups, counting together

5. Do 50 jumping jacks, counting together.

6. Do 15 push-ups, counting together.

7. Jog with your partner, right/left arms hooked at the elbows, and lightly touch 10 different people.

CHALLENGE STATIONS

Arrange various challenge stations around the perimeter of the gym. At each station place a "task card" describing the challenge activity. With partners, students move through as many stations as possible in 5–7 minutes. After both partners complete a station, they run to the card table and are given a "success card." When you give a card to a student, check off that student's name on the roll sheet.

SAMPLE STATIONS and SUCCESS CARDS

1. Can you do 60 jump rope turns in 60 seconds?

I DID 60 JUMP-ROPE TURNS IN 60 SECONDS

2. Can you juggle 3 objects continuously for 30 seconds?

I JUGGLED 3 OBJECTS CONTINUOUSLY FOR 30 SECONDS

3. Can you toss a frisbee into the target 5 out of 10 times from 25 feet away?

I TOSSED A FRISBEE INTO THE TARGET _____ OUT OF 10 TIMES

4. Can you do the ball hop between lines 30 feet apart for 60 seconds?

```
I DID THE BALL HOP CONTINUOUSLY FOR 60 SECONDS
```

5. Can you do a handstand inside a hula hoop for 10 seconds?

```
I DID A HOOP HANDSTAND FOR 10 SECONDS
```

6. Can you do 10 repetitions of the Shuttle Run between lines 30 feet apart in 60 seconds?

```
I DID 10 REPETITIONS OF THE SHUTTLE RUN IN 60 SECONDS
```

7. Can you jump in and out of a hula hoop 50 times without stopping?

```
I DID 50 CONTINUOUS JUMPS IN AND OUT OF A HULA HOOP
```

8. Can you do 15 elevated push-ups (feet on a bench)?

```
I CAN DO 15 ELEVATED PUSH-UPS
```

As students complete each challenge and receive their cards, the names can be marked off on the roll sheet. Those students not meeting the challenge come to the "card table," receive a "goal card," and have their names marked off. Students receiving a "goal card" try to reach their goal during the next day challenge stations are used.

```
MY GOAL FOR THE NEXT CHALLENGE IS:
```

PLANNING SUCCESSFUL LESSONS

If students are to achieve the highest possible level of success, they must receive instruction and activity that is purposeful, carefully planned, and implemented in a motivational and student-centered manner. Planning begins with the development of program goals and a sequential listing of activities both within and between grade levels.

CORE ACTIVITIES UNIT PLAN

Grade 4:

Balance Unit	Boards, Disc, Beams, Unicycles, Walkers
Juggling Unit	Scarves, Cubes, Balls, Flower Sticks
Leisure 1	Bowling
Leisure 2	Pickleball (basic skills)
Rhythms	Line and Folk Dance, Jump Bands
Dual and Team	Soccer, Floor Hockey, Basketball, Volleyball, Softball
Self-testing	Rope Skipping, Rope Climbing, Individual Tug-of-War Ropes
Health-Fitness	Muscular Strength, Nutrition, Fitness Goal Setting

Grade 5:

Balance Unit	Discs, Unicycles, Balance Boards, Skill Combinations (balance with other manipulatives, e.g., juggling, passing a ball)
Juggling Unit	Scarves, Rings, Clubs, Diablos
Leisure 1	Orienteering
Leisure 2	Tennis (indoor) and Golf
Rhythms	Line and "Fad" Dance
Dual and Team	Basketball, Football, Volleyball
Self-testing	Rope Skipping, Individual Challenges
Health-Fitness	Cardiovascular Endurance, Fitness Goal Setting

Grade 6:

Leisure 1	Pickleball (doubles and singles)
Rhythms	Line and Folk Dance, Jump Bands
Dual and Team	Volleyball, Soccer, Basketball, Floor Hockey, Softball
Self-testing	Juggling, Cycling
Health-Fitness	Fitness Monitoring, Diet Analysis, Physical Activity Plan Development

Grade 7:

Leisure 1	Badminton
Leisure 2	Golf
Rhythms	"Fad" Dance
Dual and Team	Basketball, Softball, Volleyball, Soccer
Health-Fitness	Body Systems Functions and Relationships, Cardiovascular Endurance, Fitness Goals

Grade 8:

Leisure 1	Tennis (indoor or outdoor)
Leisure 2	Golf
Dual and Team	Floor Hockey, Soccer, Basketball, Volleyball Team Handball
Health-Fitness	Design and Implement Personal Health and Activity Plan, Nutrition Analysis, Physical Activity Analysis

After you develop a sequential plan of activities, the next step is to develop a common presentation format. To implement a program that focuses on success for all students, each day must include a wide variety of activities that provide numerous opportunities for each student to experience personal success. Following is a brief overview of the four basic components of a success-oriented format.

PRECLASS CHALLENGES

Research and practice tell us that, when students come to physical education classes, they are prepared to be active. In order to meet this need, a low-organized and motivational activity can be provided. These activities should last for approximately 3 to 5 minutes, during which time roll may be taken or equipment set up.

Sample Activities:

1. Set up challenge stations around the gym, for example, jump ropes, juggling, pogo sticks, skill-related activities such as basketball shots, or fitness activities such as push-ups or chin-ups. Have students enter the gym, go to a station, and perform the assigned task. At the conclusion of the time limit, have them either record their score on a file card or pick up a success card.

2. Post a series of progressive stretching activities on the wall. Have students begin the stretching program as soon as they enter the facility.

Sample Activity Charts

Activity Card	Activity Card	Activity Card
Jog Laps for 3 Minutes	Challenge Stations Work Level I (Fast Pace)	Cooperative Warm-up 7 Station Rotation
Beat Your Time	*Get Your Success Card*	*Work with Your Partner*

DEVELOPMENTAL FITNESS ACTIVITIES

In addition to keeping all students active for the majority of class time, each class period should offer specific activities, of sufficient intensity and duration, to develop the basic components of health-related fitness—cardiovascular endurance, muscular strength, and flexibility. Various routines and activities, like those in Section 2, should be presented. Developmentally appropriate activities include various forms of circuit training, teacher-leader routines, and cooperative activities and challenges.

Remember that variety is the key to success. Extended periods of formal regimented exercises can, and often do, turn students away from an active and healthy lifestyle both now and in the future.

LESSON-CORE ACTIVITIES

The lesson core provides students with the opportunity to focus on sequential skill development and active participation in a variety of activities. At the intermediate and middle level, students need to be exposed to a wide variety of activities presented in short units.

CLOSING ACTIVITIES

At the close of each lesson, students have the need to participate in a low-organized activity that is also fun. This activity should be designed to provide each student with a feeling of success and enjoyment from the class. Included in this 3- to 5-minute period should be noncompetitive games, cooperation activities, quick relays, and individual or groups challenges.

STUDENT ASSISTANTS

EXPECTATIONS

The use of student assistants not only provides extra help in organization and management tasks but can also play a major roll in the instructional program. Traditionally student assistants have taken roll, checked out locks, corrected tests, arranged equipment, and led exercises. In a student-centered and success-oriented program, student assistants not only assist with management tasks but also play a major roll in providing instructional assistance to other students. The following provides an outline of appropriate and inappropriate tasks for student assistants.

Appropriate

1. Demonstrate skills to large groups.
2. Assist lower-skilled students in small groups or individually.
3. Set up equipment.
4. Refer discipline problems.
5. Act as a positive role model.

Inappropiate

1. Provide large-group instruction.
2. Be in charge of a class or group.
3. Clean storage rooms
4. Discipline other students.
5. Show off or be given "special" privileges.
6. Correct tests or record grades.

To maintain a positive and educational relationship with student assistants, you must be sure that they know what is expected. Therefore, a written "contract," which lists expectations, should be developed and signed by teachers and students.

SAMPLE STUDENT ASSISTANT CONTRACT

Physical Education
Student Assistants
EXPECTATIONS

Thanks for agreeing to assist the physical eductation staff this semester. As with all other classes you are taking, you will have to meet specific expectations. To receive a passing grade you must

1. be on time to class.

2. be dressed for activity and be ready to participate

3. behave in an appropriate manner and follow class guidelines

4. be respectful to all students and staff you are working with.

During each class you may be asked to do any of the following tasks:

1. Arrange equipment for class activity.

2. Distribute rewards and check on student progress toward achieving goals for preclass activities.

3. Lead fitness activities—stations, games, and exercises.

4. Demonstrate skills as asked by the instructor.

5. Assist students as asked by the instructor.

6. Be a positive and helpful role model for others.

If, at any time, you see another student disrupting the class, violating any class or school rules, or participating in an unsafe manner, report it to the teacher immediately.

_____   _____
Student signature   Teacher signature

Date _____

ASSESSMENT MADE EASY

Accountability and assessment are a focal point of today's programs. Fortunately, assessment for students now has a positive rather than a negative meaning. Students are now active participants in the assessment of their skills and progress toward meeting both personal and programmatic goals. These "interactive assessments" can take many different forms. The following is a brief overview of some techniques that have proven extremely successful.

VIDEO REVIEWS

Taking a page from coaching, videotape the performance of individual or small groups of students while they are participating in drills or lead-up or game activities. Have students watch the tape and critique their performance based on a standard checklist.

Skill Review Checklist
Rope Skipping

BASICS

SKILL	COMMENT	RATING (1–5)
1. Back straight		1 2 3 4 5
2. Knees slightly bent		1 2 3 4 5
3. Elbows close to side		1 2 3 4 5
4. Hands even with hips		1 2 3 4 5
General Comments:		

PEER OBSERVATIONS

Using a checklist similar to the one used for video review, have students, in groups of two, observe and critique the partner's performance. It must be remembered that both the peer and video observations are used to assist students in improving their performance—not as a method of establishing a "final" grade.

PARTICIPATION OBSERVATIONS

The goal of any physical education program is to develop or enhance students' ability so that they can actively participate—*at a recreational level*—in the activity being presented. Therefore, to determine if the goal has been accomplished, teacher observations must be made during game situations. Remember that a passing grade in a physical education class should not reflect varsity-level ability but rather the ability to participate for personal enjoyment on a recreational level.

CONCLUSION

If we are to provide all students with a positive experience in physical education and set the stage for a lifetime of physical activity, we must create a learning environment that stimulates students to think, observe, and become aware of the benefits of participating in appropriate physical activities. Each student must have daily opportunities to explore various activities and expand his or her knowledge and skill in a positive setting in which he or she can be successful. While this may mean major changes in the philosophy of some programs, it may be as simple as de-emphasizing the highly competitive situations, thus eliminating the frustration of failing, which may lead to elimination of physical activity as a positive lifestyle habit.

SECTION 2

Fitness Development

Fitness Programs

- **V**ary activities with emphasis on personal challenges and goal setting.

- **M**onitor for individual progress and modify when necessary.

- **C**ombine motor skill acquisition with fitness development.

- **S**tress health-related fitness contributing to the development of a healthy lifestyle.

Fitness Development

- Partner Scramble
- Exercise Band Aerobics
- Fitness Mixer
- Group Switch
- Moving
- Quickie Fitness Challenges
- Sideline Aerobics
- Towel Aerobics
- Fitness Circuit Challenge
- Mat Circuits

- Team Rotation
- Mass Circuit
- Football Fitness
- Basketball Fitness
- For the Record
- Fitness Poker
- Frisbee Shuttle
- Race Course
- Aerobic and Strength Invervals
- Fitness in Four

Traditionally, one of the major objectives of physical education programs has been the development of an adequate level of physical fitness. While skill development and participation in various physical activities are vital components of any quality physical education program, a well-designed physical fitness component must also be emphasized. To create the necessary emphasis, a selected amount of time during each class period must be devoted to achievement of fitness goals. During this time, students should be engaged in formalized activities designed to increase heart rates, build muscular strength and endurance, and increase flexibility.

The activities presented in this section are specifically designed for a 7–10 minute portion of a class period. Each activity provides an appropriate amount of physical activity in an enjoyable and motivational format that is easy for students and teachers to follow.

ACTIVITY: PARTNER SCRAMBLE

Focus/ Knowledge Skill	Equipment Needed	Suggested Grade Levels
Various fitness-related activities performed while cooperating with others	4–10 jump ropes 4–10 exercise bands 1–2 medicine balls Student checklist and pencils	Grades 4–7 Modifications for grade levels: The number of repetitions and activities should be modified to allow for success.

Success Notes This is an excellent activity to use at the beginning of each school year or semester. By changing partners during the station rotation, students get to know classmates and enhance their abilities to cooperate.

MAKING IT WORK

After developing the student checklist to meet the ability levels of the class, arrange stations in a random fashion within the area of a basketball court. At each station, place a brief description of the activity (as on the student checklist).

The task for students is to complete all 10 stations using at least 7 different partners. On the "go" signal, all students jog one lap. When completed, they get a partner, move to a station, complete the activity listed, and check it off their lists. After completing the activity, they jog another lap, get a new partner and complete another station.

Students continue this rotation until all have completed the entire circuit.

Sample Activities for Checklist

✔ Do 20 push-ups (list any modifications)

✔ Do 25 crunches

✔ Do 15 arm curls with an exercise band

✔ Jog 2 laps

✔ Do 30 curl-ups with medicine ball pass

✔ Do 75 jumps with a ball between your knees

✔ Jump rope for 1 minute

✔ Do 20 tricep extensions with a band

✔ Do 20 sitting presses with an exercise band

✔ Do 50 bench step-ups (steady pace)

ACTIVITY: EXERCISE BAND AEROBICS

Focus/ Knowledge Skill	Equipment Needed	Suggested Grade Levels
Enhancement of cardio-vascular endurance, combined with muscular strength and endurance	Exercise bands (Dyna Bands) for each student Tape or CD player with strong 4 count beat music	Grades 4–8 Modifications for grade levels: Utilize more advanced activities with the bands and increase the speed of rhythmic movements.

Success Notes Enhance motivation by having groups of students lead band activities and develop rhythmic movements.

MAKING IT WORK

Have students move to an open area away from others. To begin, have students slowly stretch, using their exercise bands.

- Hands held wide, stretch up and hold
- Keeping hands above head bend to the right side and hold; repeat to the left
- Back flat and knees slightly bent, bend forward and hold

As the music begins, have students step in place to the beat followed by:

- 4 steps forward
- 4 steps back
- Repeat 4 times
- 4 cross-over steps right
- 4 cross-over steps left
- Repeat 4 times

Band Activities

- 4 pulls front
- 4 pulls up right; 4 pulls up left
- Repeat 4 times

Repeat this progression for the duration of the music.

21

ACTIVITY: FITNESS MIXER

Focus/ Knowledge Skill	Equipment Needed	Suggested Grade Levels
Increase cooperation while participating in various fitness and skill development activities.	Varies, depending on area of fitness and skill development targeted Examples: 2 medicine balls; 4 jump ropes; 4 exercise bands; 4 folding mats; 12 poly-spots; 12 cone markers; 4 volleyballs; low benches/bleachers	Grades 4–8 Modifications for grade levels: Little or no record-keeping Increase time at each station up to a maximum of 1 min. 30 sec. per station.

Success Notes Set up the circuit so that there is one station for every two students in class. This allows everyone to be working at the same time. Have students go through the circuit two or more times prior to giving them written checklists. When using the checklist, make sure to move around, giving assistance and helping keep students on task.

MAKING IT WORK

Have each student find a beginning partner. When the music begins, the partners go to a station and complete the activity. After both partners complete that activity, they go to the center, find a different partner, and complete another activity. This rotation continues until all students have completed the entire circuit of activities.

Sample: A 14-station circuit—28 students with a skill focus on volleyball.

1. Bench Step	6. Medicine Ball Pass	11. Medicine Ball Crunch
2. Push-Ups	7. Shuttle Run	12. Partner Volley
3. Jump Rope	8. Gym Run	13. Poly-Spot Jump
4. Wall Volley	9. Ball Hops	14. Volleybird® Volley
5. Crunches	10. Arm Curls	

ACTIVITY: GROUP SWITCH

Focus/ Knowledge Skill	Equipment Needed	Suggested Grade Levels
General fitness development, with emphasis placed on specific components of health-related fitness as determined by choice of activities	Cone markers Equipment as needed for chosen activities Tape player or CD	Grades 4–8

Success Notes Motivate the "running" groups by posting the number of laps run in the specified time. At the conclusion of the total exercise period, add the number of laps run by each group and compare. Have students positively encourage one another to keep moving at an individual pace.

MAKING IT WORK
Place cone markers at each corner of the basketball court lines. Arrange 6 stations in the center of the gym (sample stations shown below).

Divide the class into two equal groups. Have one group go to the center while the other goes to one sideline. On signal, the sideline group begins to jog around the perimeter for 3–4 minutes. During this time, the other group begins to rotate around stations set in the center area. The rotation for the center group is 1 minute per station. After 3–4 minutes, the groups switch places and begin the rotation. Each group should run twice and do the center circuit twice. During the second rotation, the center group should do stations not done in the first rotation.

SAMPLE STATIONS

Speed skipping (jump rope)
Arm curls with exercise bands or light weights
Push-ups (use individual modifications for motivation)
Crab walk
Bench step-ups
Crunches/curl-ups

ACTIVITY: MOVING

Focus/ Knowledge Skill	Equipment Needed	Suggested Grade Levels
General fitness development	Cone markers Jump ropes Tape or CD player	Grades 4–8

Success Notes Provide age-appropriate and challenging activities for the students. This gives them continued motivation.

MAKING IT WORK

Arrange students in rows of six at one end of the gym. At the opposite end of the gym, place one cone marker for each row. The activity begins with all students performing a basic exercise routine. After approximately 30–45 seconds, call out "Moving." On that signal, all students follow their row leader and run around the cone and back, with the leader going to the end of the line, and the next person becoming the new leader. This pattern continues for 6 rotations.

MODIFICATIONS

1. Have the row leaders determine the in-line exercise each group is to perform.

2. Have one group responsible for leading the in-line exercise each rotation.

3. Have students perform different locomotor activities as they "move."

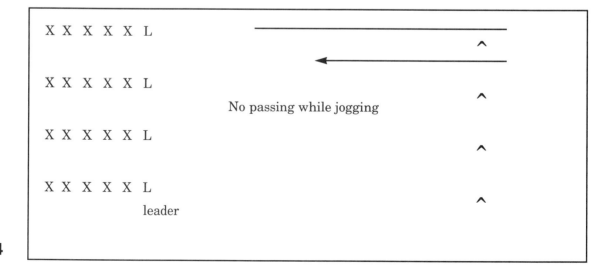

ACTIVITY: QUICKIE FITNESS CHALLENGES

Focus/ Knowledge Skill	Equipment Needed	Suggested Grade Levels
Quick fitness challenges lasting for four minutes or less	None	Grades 4–8 Modifications for grade levels: as needed by individual students based on their developmental levels.

Success Notes Reward students when they successfully complete a challenge. Posting names on the wall or giving each student a challenge card and marking off the challenges completed can do this.

MAKING IT WORK

These activities are designed to be used as quick challenges lasting for up to 4 minutes, either at the end of a class or during skill practice as a "fitness break." They also help to provide instant class management by changing to a fast-paced challenging activity in which all students can experience success.

Partner Knee Dip Partners stand facing each other joining right (left) hands. To begin, one partner lifts the right (left) leg and performs a leg "dip." Partners alternate dipping.

Push-Up Tag Partners get in push-up position facing each other about 3 inches apart. The object is to see how many times each student can touch the partner's hand within the time limit. Caution: Tell students not to pull on the arm or touch anything above the hand.

Partner Spring Partners stand facing each other approximately 2 feet apart. The object is to push against each other's hands, trying to make the partner move her or his feet.

Partner Push-Up Partners get in push-up position facing the same directions with shoulders touching. When ready, they place the inside arm on the shoulder of the partner and attempt to do a push-up.

V-Sit Press Partners of similar size sit facing each other with their feet approximately even with the hips of the partner. To begin, one partner holds the feet of the other and lifts the feet above the head, then lowers them slowly. Repeat several times, then partners switch positions.

Bottoms Up Partners of similar size sit facing each other with the soles of their feet touching and hands behind, supporting their bodies. When ready, both partners push with their feet and attempt to raise their buttocks off the ground.

Team Wall-Touch In groups of six, students form a line, facing the same direction and holding the hips of the person in front of them. On the "go" signal, students begin to run across the gym. When the last person in the group reaches the wall or a designated end line, everyone lets go, turns 180 degrees, holds the hip of the person in front, and begins to run back to the original line. Groups repeat this activity, counting the number of lines touched in the time period.

Fast Pass Divide the class into two groups, each standing on one side of the gym. The direction is given to use a specific locomotor activity. On the "go" signal, students quickly move to the other side of the gym using that activity. When they reach the other side, they jump into the air, turn 180 degrees, and clap their hands twice. When all students have reached their side, the direction is given to go again, using a different locomotor activity.

Stay Close Challenge Partners number off as 1 and 2. On the go signal, 1 attempts to run away from 2. After ten seconds, the signal to "freeze" is given. If 2 can touch 1 by taking no more than two steps, a point is awarded. Students then change roles and go again.

Partner Push-Up/Curl-Up One partner assumes a bent-knee curl-up position. The other partner places his or her hands on the feet of the partner, assuming a push-up position. As one partner completes a curl-up, the other partner follows with a push-up.

ACTIVITY: SIDELINE AEROBICS

Focus/ Knowledge Skill	Equipment Needed	Suggested Grade Levels
General fitness development, with activities designed to target specific health-related fitness areas	Equipment is based on the activities presented. Tape or CD player with motivational music	Grades 5–8 Modifications can be related made in the duration and intensity of each activity presented. Individual modifications can be made to accommodate student abilities.

Success Notes Participate actively in leading the class in the general aerobic portion of the workout. Keep students moving and motivated by adding challenging activities and movements to both the general aerobic portion and the sideline portions.

MAKING IT WORK

The routine begins with all students grouped in the center of the facility. To begin, lead an aerobic type activity for 1 minute. At the conclusion of the aerobic minute, students move, using a specified locomotor movement—skip, gallop, hop, jump—to "Sideline 1." At that station, lead the students in a specified activity for 30–45 seconds. Students then repeat the locomotor activity and regroup in the center for another 1 minute of aerobic activity. Continue the pattern until all four sideline activities have been completed.

Modification:

Shorten the center aerobic activity to 30 seconds and go to each sideline twice, changing activities each time.

Sample Sideline Activities:

"Sideline 1:"   Crab Walk
                Curl-Ups
                Push-Ups

"Sideline 2:"   Jumping Jacks
                Skier Jumps
                Rope Skipping

"Sideline 3:"   Bench Step-Ups
                Over-the-line Push-Ups
                Speed Rope

"Sideline 4:"   Band Curls
                Running 1 lap
                Bench/Chair Dips

ACTIVITY: TOWEL AEROBICS

Focus/ Knowledge Skill	Equipment Needed	Suggested Grade Levels
General fitness development, with emphasis placed on specific health-related components using focused activities	One towel (carpet squares can be substituted) for each student Tape or CD player	Grades 6–8

Success Notes Use your, and the students', imagination to create interesting and challenging routines.

MAKING IT WORK

Have each student take a towel to an open area of the gym, stand by it, and get ready to begin the routine. The routine may begin with teacher-directed activities and change to student- or student leader-directed as the class gains in knowledge and abilities.

Sample Routine:

- Stand beside towel and stretch.

- Stand on the towel and twist.

- Slide on the towel, place feet on the outside edges and move feet together and apart.

- Put hands on the towel and push it around the floor.

- In "crab-walk" position, with feet on the towel, move the towel around the floor.

- Jump on and off and side to side.

- Stand on one side and jump on; jump off to the other side.

- With one foot on and one foot off, push the towel around the room.

- From a push-up position, with feet on the towel and hands off, move around the room.

- Sit on the towel and move around, "pulling" with feet.

- With both feet on the towel, move feet forward and back, alternating feet.

ACTIVITY: FITNESS CIRCUIT CHALLENGE

Focus/ Knowledge Skill	Equipment Needed	Suggested Grade Levels
Contains a number of activities designed to increase fitness levels and enhance skill; can be used as a warm-up, but it is suggested that it be used as a lesson focus	Equipment is determined by individual school inventories Example: "fitness ball," jump ropes, jumping boxes, poly-spots, scooter boards, balls, incline mat, jump balls	Grades 4–8 Modifications for grade levels: Adjust the equipment to meet the needs of the students involved.

Success Notes Make the circuit both challenging and fun

MAKING IT WORK

Arrange stations throughout the facility, providing enough space for safe activity. Each station should accommodate three to four students participating at the same time. On the "go" signal, students begin the activity at their station and continue until the "stop" signal. At that time, they all rotate in a clockwise direction to the next station.

The uniqueness of this circuit is found in the equipment used. It combines traditional fitness activities with challenging fitness/skill activities. Following is a description of this circuit.

Station 1: **Incline Cage Ball Push**—Place one end of a portable balance beam on one or two folded mats. Students, in a cooperative effort, push a cage ball up the incline and off the high end. They then roll it to a line 15 feet away, pick it up, carry it back to the start, and repeat the activity.

Station 2: **Scooter Board Pull**—Place a heavy rope between two volleyball standards approximately 3 feet off the ground. Students lie on two scooter boards, lower backs on one and feet on the other, take hold of the rope, and pull themselves to the other end where they exchange with a partner.

Station 3: **Jumping Boxes**—Place five jumping boxes or folded mats (12 to 24 inches high) approximately 3 feet apart, followed by eight to ten poly-spots approximately 1 foot apart. Students begin by jumping on the first box, to the floor, to the next box, and so on. After the last box, they jump from poly-spot to poly-spot until the course is completed. They then wait for the other group members to finish, and reverse the course.

29

Station 4: **Fitness Ball Slide**—A "fitness ball" is a solid ball with a tube running through the center. A cord, running through the center, is stretched between two volleyball standards approximately 15 feet apart. Students stand by the standards and push the ball between them.

Station 5: **Jump Rope Pyramid**—Students begin jumping at a steady pace of approximately 100 turns per minute (TPM). At 30-second intervals they increase the TPM by 20 until they reach 160 TPM for 2 minutes. At that stage, they reverse the pattern and return to the 100 TPM baseline. Rest for 1 minute and repeat the pyramid twice.

Station 6: **Ball Hop**— Students place a volleyball between their knees and hop from a starting line to another approximately 20 feet away. Do 10 push-ups and return to the start line; do 15 curl-ups and return to the push-up line. The progression continues for 10 rotations. Students rest for 1 minute and repeat.

Station 7: **Tennis Ball Drop-(Quick Hands)**— Student 1 stands on a chair or bleachers with a partner (student 2) standing in front of her or him, hands on hips. Partner 1 drops a tennis ball from chin height. Partner 2 attempts to catch it. For more advanced students, partner 1 should drop two balls at the same time.

Students should remain at each station for 5–7 minutes. At the conclusion of time, all students run 1 lap, stopping at the station to the right of their starting point.

ACTIVITY: MAT CIRCUITS

Focus/ Knowledge Skill	Equipment Needed	Suggested Grade Levels
General fitness activities or specific activities targeted to increase certain components of health-related fitness	5´ × 10´ or 4´ × 8´ folding mats for each group of 4 or 5 students 1 or 2 jump ropes per mat	Grades 4–8 Modifications for grade levels: Allow for the use of individual variations when doing push-ups and curl-ups/crunches.

Success Notes Use lively music during the exercise phase of this activity. Allow for a 5–10-second rotation between stations. Make sure that, when you arrange the stations, the push-up and curl-up/crunch stations are located at the ends of the mat; this keeps the mat from sliding.

MAKING IT WORK

Place folded mats in various locations throughout the gym. Place one jump rope at each mat. Divide students into groups of four, and assign each group to a mat.

Each mat has four stations, depending on the number of students assigned.

SIDE 1—Step-up　　　　　　SIDE 2—Jump Rope (to side of mat)

END 1—Push-Up　　　　　　END 2—Curl-Ups or Crunches

NOTE: If additional students are assigned to each mat, then two students can be assigned to each station.

On the "go" signal (music begins) students begin to perform the activity at the station assigned.

- **Step-Up**—stepping up and down at a steady pace
- **Push-Up**—hands or feet on the mat doing continuous push-ups
- **Curl-Up**—feet on the mat, knees bent doing crunches or curl-ups
- **Jump Rope**—continuous jumping

After the designated time—1 to 2 minutes—the signal is given to rotate one station to the right. After a 5-second pause the signal to begin is given. This rotation continues until students have completed each station.

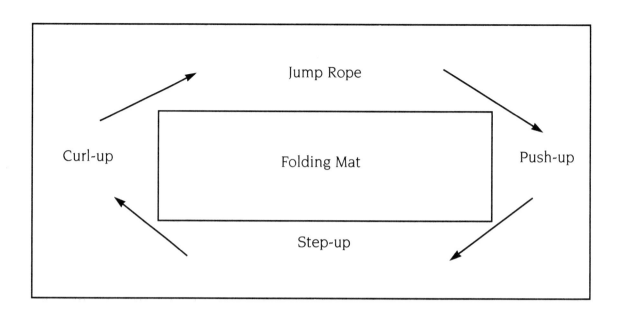

ACTIVITY: TEAM ROTATION

Focus/ Knowledge Skill	Equipment Needed	Suggested Grade Levels
Increase fitness and skill levels of students	8 poly-spots or cone markers Task cards for each station Equipment necessary for stations	Grades 4–8 Modifications for grade levels: Adjust activities to meet fitness and skill level of students participating.

Success Notes Tasks for each station should be age-appropriate for the class. Rather than using a specified number of repetitions at each station, rotation should be based on a given period of time.

MAKING IT WORK

Place a line of eight poly-spots or cone markers, evenly spaced, on one side of the facility. At each marker place a task card listing the activity to be completed at that station. Any equipment necessary should be placed beside the markers. Make sure enough equipment is at each station to allow members of each team to participate.

Have students divide into groups of eight. Each group should form a relay line with one member opposite each marker. On the "go" signal, students perform the task listed at their marker. After the given time period, all team members move up one station with the front members moving to the back. This rotation continues until all members of each group have completed each station.

SAMPLE TASKS

Rope Skipping	Push-Ups	Crunches	Jumping Jacks
Run Laps	Kick Through	Skier Jumps	Walk-Line Push-Ups

ACTIVITY: MASS CIRCUIT

Focus/ Knowledge Skill	Equipment Needed	Suggested Grade Levels
20-minute fitness circuit—provides a total body workout, with emphasis on the enhancement of cardiovascular endurance.	Step benches/bleachers, light dumbbells, exercise stationary bikes, scooter boards, jump ropes, cone markers, basketballs, folding mats	Grades 6–8 Modifications for grade levels: Lower the amount of time spent at each station for younger students.

Success Notes Have students keep track of the repetitions done at each station. With each successive time the activity is presented, have each individual establish a "personal best" for that station. This activity should be used in conjunction with the Physical Fitness Study Guides (see Section 5); it works best if presented at least two times per week.

MAKING IT WORK

This format places an emphasis on fitness development while providing opportunities for students to set goals and develop an understanding of the importance of physical fitness to one's life.

Arrange ten fitness stations around the gym. After 3–4 minutes of stretching, assign two or three students to each station. On the "go" signal, all students begin 2–3 minutes of activity. At the conclusion of the time, the signal to rotate is given, students are given 15 seconds to rotate to the next station before the "go" signal is given. The rotation continues until all stations have been completed. If recording scores, allow 30 seconds between stations. After all stations have been completed, students walk 1 lap of the gym followed by 3 minutes of slow stretching.

Sample Circuit:

Ball Pass/Curl Up	Scooter Pull	Stationary Bikes
Jump Rope	Dumbbell Curl	Dumbbell Rowing
Bench Step	Exercise Bands	Curl-Ups/Crunches
	Agility Run	

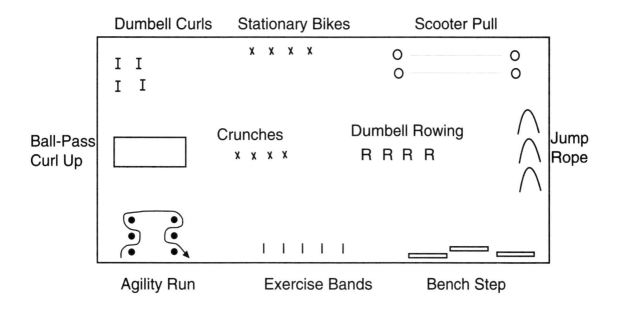

Sample Circuit Activities

Ball Pass/Curl Up: Each student, with a ball, lies on back with knees bent, feet toward the wall. As students begin doing a curl-up, the ball is passed to the wall; when catching the rebound, students lower themselves back to the start position.

Scooter Pull: Using a gym scooter, students sit, lie, or kneel on a scooter and move—using arms, legs, or a combination—from one side of the area to the other. A great variation is to tie a rope between two volleyball standards, approximately 2 feet off the ground, and have the students lie on their backs and pull themselves between standards.

Stationary Bikes: Students ride the stationary bikes for the duration.

Jump Rope: Students jump rope continuously for the duration.

Dumbbell Curl: Sitting in a chair or on a bench, do bent arm curls using light-weight dumbbells.

Dumbbell Rowing: Standing with back against a wall, perform an "upright" rowing movement, bringing each dumbbell to a position underneath the chin and back down to the sides.

Bench Step: Using either Aerobic Steps or bleachers, students rhythmically step up and down for the time period.

Exercise Bands: Using an exercise band, pull arms apart and together, up and down, in a rhythmic pattern for the time period.

Curl-Up/Crunch: Lying on a mat, students individually do crunches and/or curl-ups for the time period. Remind students to keep to a 3 second beat—up 1, hold 1, down 1.

Agility Run: Using cone markers, set an agility run course. Students run through the course, then go straight back to the start and repeat the pattern.

35

ACTIVITY: FOOTBALL FITNESS

Focus/ Knowledge Skill	Equipment Needed	Suggested Grade Levels
Cardiovascular fitness is enhanced as well as cooperative skills, and skills used in football.	12 cone markers Poly-spot markers 6 milk crates or 12″ × 12″ boxes 1 scooter board 10 bean bags 6 footballs String, tape, or sticks to place between cones for hurdles 28 jump ropes	Grade 5–8 Modifications for grade levels: The time at each station should be increased with grade levels: 1 minute for grade 5 up to 2 minutes for grade 8.

Success Notes This is an excellent activity to build football skills and enhance fitness levels. Allow groups several opportunities at the skill stations to give all students equal opportunity to attempt the task.

MAKING IT WORK

Arrange seven stations around the gym area, allowing enough space for each activity. At each station, place a cone with an activity task card attached. Assign a group of four students to each station. On the "go" signal, students begin the activity listed for the time period. At the conclusion of the time period, all students pick up a jump rope and jump for 30 seconds, then rotate to the next station. This format is repeated until all stations are completed.

Football Fitness Stations

1. **Accuracy Toss:** Students toss bean bags from the start line into 12″ × 12″ boxes placed in a row in front of them. After tossing into the closest box, they attempt to toss into the next box. They keep tossing until they have landed a toss in each box or had 10 attempts.

2. **Over-Under:** In a relay fashion, students move through the course of hurdles, going over the first, under the second, over the third, under the fourth, and so on.

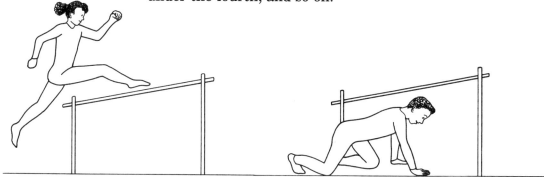

3. **Scooter Push:** One student sits on a scooterboard with his or her partner standing on a line. The scooter person pushes out and catches a pass (football or bean bag) thrown by the partner.

4. **Hand-Off:** 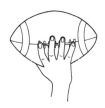 Each member of the group takes a beginning position as a center, quarterback, runner, or returnee. The center give the ball to the quarterback who "pitches" it to the runner. The runner then takes the ball to a mark 20 yards ahead and hands it to the returner, who runs it back to the line. After each run, players switch positions (center to quarterback, quarterback to runner, runner to returner, and returner to center).

5. **Shuttle Run:** Group members run between lines 30 feet apart. On the "go" signal, they run from the start line to the next line, touch it with the hand, return to the start line, touch it, and return. This rotation continues for the duration.

6. **Rotation Passing:** Each member of the group takes a beginning position as a center, quarterback, receiver, or returner. The center gives the ball to the quarterback, who passes to the receiver. The receiver then passes to the returner. After each pass, the players rotate positions; center to quarterback, quarterback to receiver, receiver to returner. (This activity can be made more challenging by having the players stay in their positions as they see how many passes can be completed in a specified amount of time.)

7. **Speed Skip:** Each group member takes a jump rope and on signal begins to jump for speed. The total number of jumps in the time limit is the score.

ACTIVITY: BASKETBALL FITNESS

Focus/ Knowledge Skill	Equipment Needed	Suggested Grade Levels
Cardiovascular fitness is enhanced as well as jumping skills and various ball-control and defensive skills used in basketball.	17 cone markers each Activity task cards for each station (8) Basketballs for skill stations. Tape or stick to place between cones	Grades 4–8 Modifications for grade levels: The time at each station should be increased with grade levels: 20 seconds for grade 4 up to 1 minute for grade 8.

Success Notes Stress continued activity and improvement of skills. Students also become motivated through the use of activity cards on which they record the number of jumps they and a partner do at each station.

MAKING IT WORK

Arrange eight stations around the outside of a basketball court. At each station, place a cone with an activity task card attached. Assign a group of students to each station. On the "go" signal, students begin the activity listed for the time period. At the conclusion of the time period, all students do 15 seconds of push-ups or crunches and then rotate to the next station. This format is repeated until all stations are completed.

Sample Stations

1. Skier jump across the line
2. Vertical jump (record the height of each jump and add the total)
3. Jump rope
4. Jump forward and back over the line
5. Figure 8 dribble
6. Hurdle jump (jump over a tape/stick placed between 2 cones)
7. Wall pass (standing 4 feet from a wall, perform a chest pass into the wall and catch the return)
8. Rebound and shoot (bounce a ball off the backboard, jump, rebound, and shoot while still in the air)

ACTIVITY: FOR THE RECORD

Focus/ Knowledge Skill	Equipment Needed	Suggested Grade Levels
Recording a variety of activities in which students will participate, both in class and outside of school	"For the Record" worksheet Task cards for each activity to be presented	Grades 6–8 Modifications for grade levels: Modify activities so they are age appropriate.

Success Notes Limit the activities to those that most students can easily participate in without specialized equipment or that require several partners to accomplish. Provide feedback and check for participation on a regular basis. This is an excellent activity to integrate with goal setting lessons.

MAKING IT WORK

Arrange the gym into three major areas: (1) Aerobic Endurance and Skill Enhancement (2) Muscular Strength and Endurance (3) Flexibility and Skill Development. Each of these major areas should be divided into four stations each with a specific task card.

> Example—Aerobic Endurance and Skill Development Area:
> Station 1: Bench Step-Ups—Basketball Dribble—Soccer Dribble
> Station 2: Jump Rope for Endurance—Step Aerobics—Dance
> Station 3: Jump Rope Single Routine—Jump Rope Partner routine
> Station 4: PACER Run—Continuous Jogging—Tennis Volleying

While at the major area, students participate in one activity from each station that they would like to continue doing, both during and outside of class. They write down the title of the activity and a brief description on their worksheet. After approximately 10 minutes groups rotate to different "major areas."

Students keep their worksheets and record the dates and times they participate in the activity besides the title and description.

Modification: Have students complete only 1 major area per week. This allows them to spend more time at each station trying different activities before making a commitment to one.

For the Record

Recorded activities you will do on a regular basis. Describe the activity.

Aerobic Endurance and Skill Enhancement:

Station 1 _____

Station 2 _____

Station 3 _____

Station 4 _____

Muscular Strength and Endurance:

Station 1 _____

Station 2 _____

Station 3 _____

Station 4 _____

Flexibility and Skill Development:

Station 1 _____

Station 2 _____

Station 3 _____

Station 4 _____

ACTIVITY: FITNESS POKER

Focus/ Knowledge Skill	Equipment Needed	Suggested Grade Levels
A variety of fitness-related activities, combined in a fast-moving cooperative activity	1 deck of playing cards for each group of 5 1 set of "Fitness Poker" activity cards Jump ropes, hula hoops, volleyballs, exercise bands, cone markers, folding mats, aerobic steps	Grades 5–8

Success Notes Place various skill activities in the "activity" deck along with several "pass" cards. If a "pass" card is drawn, the group gets a free turn and deals again.

MAKING IT WORK

Divide the class into groups of five to six students each, and assign to an area of the gym. Give each group a deck of playing cards, a set of "Fitness Poker" activity cards, and appropriate equipment to accomplish activities.

On the "go" signal, one student deals the playing cards face down to each group member. After all cards are dealt, the dealer turns over an activity card, and all players turn their cards over. At that point, all students begin performing the number of repetitions as shown on their cards; face cards are worth 12, an ace is worth 15, and all number cards are worth the stated value. After completing the activity, cards are placed in a discard pile and the procedure is repeated. Try going through the playing card deck twice in 5–7 minutes.

Sample "Fitness Poker" Activity Cards

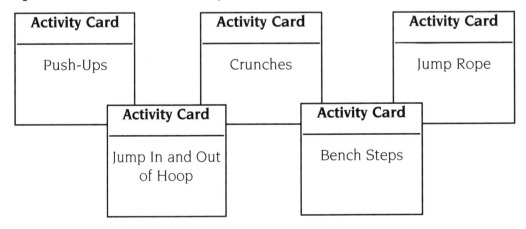

| Fitness Activities | Skill Development | Games That Teach | Healthy Lifestyles | Keeping Track |

ACTIVITY: FRISBEE SHUTTLE

Focus/ Knowledge Skill	Equipment Needed	Suggested Grade Levels
Cooperative activity—involves throwing a frisbee accurately, running, and doing designated fitness activities.	1 frisbee and 1 cone marker for each group of 4 students	Grades 4–8 Modifications for grade levels: Shorten the area to be covered for younger students; e.g., 25 yds.

Success Notes This is a great cooperative activity involving the skill of throwing a frisbee. To ensure success for all, teach frisbee-throwing skills prior to doing this activity. The better and the more accurate the throws, the more success students will experience. Encourage the use of cooperative skills to assist teammates having difficulty throwing.

MAKING IT WORK

Assign each group of four to a position on a starting line facing a cone marker placed approximately 50 yards away. On the "go" signal, the first student in each group throws the frisbee toward the opposite side; the entire group runs to the landing site where the next person throws. This rotation pattern continues until one partner hits the cone marker. After the cone has been hit, the frisbee is picked up and the entire group returns to the starting line, doing a designated activity followed by another throwing and running relay toward the target.

Sample "Start Line" Activities

Can your team do 100 jumping jacks?	Can your team do 40 push-ups?
Can each member do 20 curl-ups?	Can your team do 50 hop-line push-ups?
Can each member do 30 jump-rope turns?	Can your team do 200 jump-rope turns?

ACTIVITY: RACE COURSE

Focus/ Knowledge Skill	Equipment Needed	Suggested Grade Levels
Cardiovascular fitness and muscular strength are enhanced through this activity	None	Grades 4–8

Success Notes Keep students rotating through this fast moving activity as quickly as possible. It is suggested that only two "challenge' tasks be given for each lap.

MAKING IT WORK

Divide the class into groups of four, each group standing behind a cone in the center of the gym, facing, in relay formation, the sideline. On the "go" signal, the first student in each group begins to run the perimeter of the gym, and the remaining students in each line begin doing jumping jacks.

As the students are running the perimeter and doing jumping jacks, call out one of the signals listed below. When the signal is given, all students immediately stop and perform the activity associated with the signal. After approximately 15 seconds, give the "go" signal and students resume their aerobic activity.

After completing 1 lap the runner tags the hand of the next person in their group who begins to run. This rotation continues until everyone has had 2 or 3 turns as the runner.

Sample Activity Signals

Spin Out	Push-Ups	Out of Gas	Mountain Climbers
Flat Tire	Crunches	Red Light	Crab Walk to Center
Oil Leak	Jumping Jacks	Yellow Light	Balance on One Foot

Note: This is a modification of "Autobahn" as published in *Elementary P.E. Teachers Survival Guide* by Carpenter and Tunnell, Parker Publishing Company, West Nyack, NY, 1994.

ACTIVITY: AEROBIC AND STRENGTH INTERVALS

Focus/ Knowledge Skill	Equipment Needed	Suggested Grade Levels
Intervals provide short, high-intensity activity followed by a lower-intensity period. Both aerobic and strength-training activities are combined in this format.	Jump ropes, aerobic steps, dumbbells, and exercise bands	Grades 6–8 Modifications for grade levels: Lower-intensity activities of shorter duration should be used for younger students.

Success Notes Make sure the entire class begins at one time and that all directions are explained clearly—when a partner is needed, how to rotate, how to do the activities at each area. Keeps students moving at all times, and reinforce cooperation among group members.

MAKING IT WORK

Arrange the gym into six exercise stations, place the necessary equipment at each station, and place one cone at one sideline and another at the opposite side. Assign equal groups of students to each station.

On the "go" signal, students begin doing high-intensity repetitions of the activity assigned to their station. After 60–75 seconds of continuous repetitions, the "jog" signal is given, and the group begins a slow jog around the cones at their area. After 45–60 seconds, the groups rotate one station to their right, with the group on the far right moving to the far left. Continue the rotating stations until all groups have worked at each station.

45

ACTIVITY: FITNESS IN FOUR

Focus/ Knowledge Skill	Equipment Needed	Suggested Grade Levels
This activity is an excellent fitness motivator that can be used either as a warm-up or as a lesson-core fitness break. The concept can make use of a variety of fitness- and skill-related activities.	Jump ropes, poly-spots	Grades 4–8

Success Notes Keep the activities moving at a fast pace. Students should not be given a break between activities—keep it continuous for 4 minutes.

MAKING IT WORK

Before beginning the activity, have the students find their beginning pulse rate (take pulse for 6 seconds and add a "0"). On the "go" signal, all students begin the first activity as directed. After 20 seconds, they begin the next activity. This sequence continues for a total of 12 activities. At the completion of 4 minutes, have the students take their pulse rate again and note the difference. A cool-down of slow stretching activities should follow, lasting 1 or 2 minutes.

Sample Activities

Jumping Jacks	Push-Ups
Curl-Ups	Mountain Climbers
Crunches	Rope Jumping
Crab Kicks	Jogging in Place
Hand Walk Over a Line	Skier Jump Over a Line
Can-Can Kicks	Crab Walk

SECTION 3

Skill Development and Lead-Up Activities

SKILL CHALLENGES AND MOTIVATORS

- Activities, drills, and games must be developmentally and age appropriate.

- Individual challenges and station work provide motivation and individualization.

- Lead-up activities and games refine specific skills in simple formats.

- Cooperation and teamwork are emphasized above competition.

Basketball

Information for You

STUDY GUIDE FOR BASKETBALL

HISTORY

Basketball is the result of an experiment conducted by Dr. J.A. Naismith to develop an indoor game to fill in the seasons between football and baseball. When he developed the game in 1891–1892, Dr. Naismith used peach baskets as goals and a football for a ball.

After the first two years of playing basketball, many changes took place. During the first years, as many as fifty players made up one team. This number was reduced to nine, then seven in 1893. In 1894, the number of players was reduced to five. Another interesting change came in the way each game was started. At first, the ball was simply tossed down the center of the floor between the teams, who were lined up on either side. When the whistle blew, players from both sides ran toward the center. The first team to reach the ball retained possession.

This was one game that girls were able to take part in. As many women played the game, women's rules were developed in 1899. These rules included having the court divided into three parts; players were limited to two bounces before they had to pass or shoot.

BASIC RULES

1. There must be 5 players on each team to begin the game.

2. Substitutions are unlimited during the game.

3. The ball is put into play by a jump ball in the center of the court.

4. The team in possession of the ball is the offensive team; the other is on defense.

5. The court is divided into two equal parts.

6. Jump balls are taken whenever two players tie up a ball by one player's placing one or both hands firmly on the ball when it is already held by an opponent.

7. Player may throw, bat, bounce, hand, or roll, the ball.

8. A free throw (an unguarded shot at the basket from the foul line) scores one point. The player who was fouled must take the shot.

9. If the free throw is missed and the ball does not hit the rim, it is a violation and the other team gets the ball out-of-bounds.

10. A violation is an infringement for which the ball is put into play from out-of-bounds at the sideline. Examples are tapping the ball more than two times on a jump ball or playing the ball before it has touched the floor.

11. Kicking, striking the ball, dribbling illegally (double dribble), holding the ball longer than five seconds, causing the ball to go out-of-bounds, touching the boundary line with the body while in possession of the ball, and traveling are all violations.

12. Fouls are infringements of a rule for which one or more free throws are given. They involve physical contact between two opponents.

   - Individual fouls include pushing, holding, tripping, pulling or spinning an opponent off balance, hacking, and roughness.

   - Offensive individual fouls result when the player with the ball moves his or her body into an opponent who has a position already established.

   - Blocking fouls involve contact that impedes the progress of an opponent with or without the ball—entering the path of a moving player, guarding an opponent by holding both arms fully extended, or guarding an opponent too closely from the rear so that contact results when the player attempts to turn or pivot.

ACTIVITY: BASKETBALL SKILL DRILLS

Focus/ Knowledge Skill	Equipment Needed	Suggested Grade Levels
Basketball skills of shooting, rebounding, dribbling, passing, and defense are combined in challenging activities that are also fun.	1 basketball for each group of students Poly-spot markers	Grades 4–8 Modifications for grade levels: Lower basket height and provide opportunities for younger and smaller students to use a smaller ball.

Success Notes These drills provide for specific practice, but they should also be fun and challenging, for example, How many can you/your team do? Give rewards for individual/team effort, not score.

MAKING IT WORK

Shooting Drills

Spot Shot: Place poly spot markers in various locations around a basket. Have players take shots from each spot, and then pass the ball to the next player in line. Award the team 1 point for each basket made.

Pivot and Shoot: Using the same space arrangement as in "spot shot" have students pivot once to the right and once to the left before shooting.

Dribble and Shoot: Have groups of four to six players—each with a ball—standing at midcourt facing a basket. On signal, the first player dribbles to a spot and attempts a shot, gets the rebound, and passes to the next player in the line. If the previous shot was made, the next player may not shoot from that spot. Play continues until a shot has been made from each spot.

Sideline Lay-Up: Teams of four to six—each with a ball—stand on the sides of the key at each basket. On the "go" signal, the player farthest away from the basket dribbles down the center and attempts a layup, gets the rebound, passes to the next person in line, and goes to the end of the line. The rotation continues until each person has attempted three shoots; teams then switch sides and play begins again.

51

| *Pass and Shoot:* | Groups of two—each with a ball—stand at midcourt, approximately 10 feet from each other, and facing a basket. On the "go" signal, the students begin slowly moving toward the basket, maintaining their spacing, and pass the ball between them. When one player is near the basket, that player takes a shot and the other rebounds, then return to the end of the line. Focus on not taking steps while holding the ball. |

Dribbling and Passing

| *Hula Hoop Dribble:* | In groups of two, one person has a basketball and the other holds a jump rope tied to a hula hoop. On the "go" signal, the person holding the rope slowly begins to pull the hoop across the floor while the partner tries to maintain a correct dribble, keeping the ball inside the hoop. The person pulling the hoop may move in different directions but should move in a way to allow for success by the person dribbling. |
| *Pass and Run:* | In groups of two—each with a ball—partners stand facing each other at the midcourt line 10 feet apart. On the "go" signal, players begin passing the ball back and forth using chest, bounce, and overhead passes. On the "run" signal, the player with the ball lays it down, and both players run from their position to the end line behind them, return to the ball, and begin passing. |

Defense

| *Defend Your Lane:* | Divide the playing area into four lanes approximately 10″–12″ in width and 25′ in length. Assign four to six students to each lane, each lane with one ball. On the "go" signal, the first two players enter the lane. The first is on defense, the second offense. While staying in the lane, the offensive player attempts to move the length of the floor, and the defensive player tries to stop the dribble or force the opponent out of the lane. All regular defensive rules apply. |

| Fitness Activities | Skill Development | Games That Teach | Healthy Lifestyles | Keeping Track |

ACTIVITY: SHOOT AND RUN FOR FUN

Focus/ Knowledge Skill	Equipment Needed	Suggested Grade Levels
Basketball shooting and rebounding skills combined with fitness challenges	1 basket and 1 basketball for each group of 5–7 students 1 poly-spot or cone marker for each group Fitness Spot Cards and necessary equipment	Grades 4–8 Modifications for grade levels Use adjustable basket heights, with grade 4 students playing on an 8-hoop, grade 5 on a 9-foot hoop, and grade 6 on a 10-foot hoop.

Success Notes This is an excellent activity that keeps all students actively involved. Reinforcement of fitness activities and completion of all activities keep students on task and involved. Keep a running score of baskets made by each team.

MAKING IT WORK

Students are divided into groups—each at a basket in a single line at the free-throw line. On the "go" signal, the first player in each group attempts a free throw. If it is missed, the shooter rebounds the ball, passes to the next player in line, and returns to the end of the line. If made, all players run to a designated "fitness spot" and complete the first activity listed. After the entire group has completed the activity, they return to their basket. While the nonshooters are at the fitness area, the shooter continues to shot and rebound.

When all players have returned the next person in line shots the free throw. Students must keep the same playing order throughout the activity.

Sample Fitness Spot Cards

Activity 1:   Crab walk 20 feet and do 10 push-ups.

Activity 2:   Do 20 "slow" crunches.

Activity 3:   Jump rope for 30 seconds; try 3 different steps.

Activity 4:   Run 1 lap of the gym.

Activity 5:   Do 15 push-ups.

Activity 6:   Lift 1 leg and do a hamstring stretch for 15 seconds; repeat with the other leg.

Activity 7:   Do 15 curl-ups.

53

ACTIVITY: BASKETBALL GOLF

Focus/ Knowledge Skill	Equipment Needed	Suggested Grade Levels
Basketball shooting, dribbling, and rebounding skills, combined in a challenging activity	1 basketball for each group of 4 students Hula hoops, cone markers, jump ropes, poly-spots "Basketball Golf" score cards and a pencil for each group	Grades 4–8 Modifications for grade levels: Use adjustable basket heights, with grade 4 students playing on an 8-hoop, grade 5 on a 9-foot hoop, and grade 6 on a 10-foot hoop.

Success Notes This fun and challenging activity is best presented in a non-competitive format that stresses ball control. Individual students' success should be recognized above final scores.

MAKING IT WORK

The goal of this activity is to score the lowest number of points in completing the designated course. Each player or group has a ball. The course is laid out using all available baskets and other shooting targets. Each hole should have several obstacles, such as hula hoops or jump ropes, placed in the playing area.

SAMPLE HOLE DESIGN

"Tee Box"   BASKET

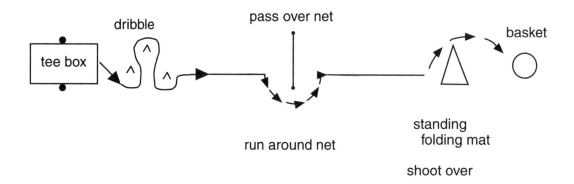

Using a "shotgun start" format (players begin on all baskets), one student in each group takes a shot from the "tee box." After the shot, each player gets the rebound and takes a second shot from where she or he gains control. If an "obstacle" is in the way the player must shoot under, over, or through it. If a ball touches an "obstacle," a point penalty is given. Play continues until a basket is scored or 5 shots have been attempted (the maximum individual score per hole is 5). Only one player from each team may be playing a hole at one time. However, other teams may be playing the same hole. If a player or the ball touches another ball, a 2-point penalty is given.

Note: Alternative baskets may be designed by taping hula hoops to the wall.

SAMPLE COURSE DESIGN

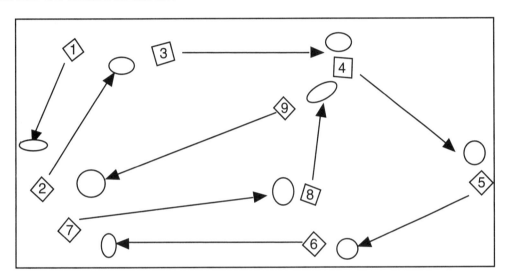

BASKETBALL GOLF SCORE CARD

Player	1	2	3	4	5	6	7	8	9	10	total

Signed: _____, _____

_____, _____

ACTIVITY: BASKETBALL NUMBERS GAME

Focus/ Knowledge Skill	Equipment Needed	Suggested Grade Levels
Basketball shooting, passing, dribbling, and rebounding skills	1 basket, 1 basketball for each group of 4–5 students 2 poly-spot or cone markers for each group	Grades 4–8 Modifications for grade levels: Use adjustable basket heights, with grade 4 students playing on an 8-foot hoop, grade 5 on a 9-foot hoop, and grade 6 on a 10-foot hoop.

Success Notes This is an excellent activity that keeps all students actively involved. Emphasis should be placed on using proper skill when passing, dribbling, and shooting. To ensure that all students are challenged, consider ability-grouping students, making the "shot spots" at different locations, depending on the group's ability.

MAKING IT WORK

Divide the class into groups of four to five students assigning each group to a basket. Players stand two on each side of the key (if five students are in a group, one should be on the foul line).

Each student should be given a number 1–4 (5).

On the "go" signal, players start passing the ball around within their group. You can either select the type of pass to be used or let students choose. After approximately 10–15 seconds of passing, call out a number. The ball is passed to that student, who dribbles to a "shot spot" and attempts a shot. If the basket is made, the group is awarded 3 points. If missed, the group gets 1 point for the attempt. The shooter gets the rebound and returns to his or her space to begin passing.

Continue calling numbers until all students have had at least three or more attempts.

Note: To involve an additional activity, have students do a fitness routine—5 push-ups, 10 curl-ups, and 20 treadmills after each shot.

ACTIVITY: BASKETBALL BEANBAG ROBBERY

Focus/ Knowledge Skill	Equipment Needed	Suggested Grade Levels
Practice in the skills of dribbling, along with refinement of hand-eye coordination and agility	5 hula hoops 4 basketballs 27 beanbags	Grades 4–7

Success Notes Remind students to watch out for others when moving and to keep a continuous count of beanbags in their hoop.

MAKING IT WORK

Using half of a basketball court, place 1 hula hoop in each corner. Have students make equal groups, facing the center, behind each hoop. In the center of the area, place 27 bean bags.

Using a relay format, each team sends students, dribbling a basketball, to the center to get a beanbag and bring it back to their hoop. When one person returns, the next one goes to the center and brings back another beanbag. When all beanbags are gone from the center, players may go to another group's hoop and take one beanbag (players may not guard beanbags). Play continues until one team gets 30 beanbags in their hoop.

Modifications:
Change the total number of beanbags in the center or the total needed to win in order to lengthen or shorten the game.

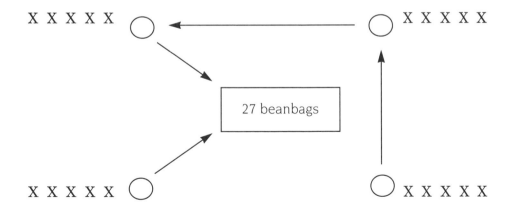

ACTIVITY: BASKETBALL CHASE

Focus/ Knowledge Skill	Equipment Needed	Suggested Grade Levels
Various passing skills and dribbling—through the use of modifications, the fitness areas of muscular strength and endurance can also be added.	1 basketball for each group of 4 students 1 poly-spot or cone marker for each student	Grades 4–6

Success Notes When arranging the playing areas, provide enough space between groups to allow for students to run safely around their area while dribbling. Stress using proper form in passing and dribbling. This should not be considered a race but a challenge to see which group can complete all passes and dribbling by each student without mishandling the ball.

MAKING IT WORK

A group of four students form a rectangle, each standing on a poly-spot or marker approximately 10–12 feet apart. On signal, players begin passing the basketball to one another using either a chest, bounce, or overhead pass. On the next signal, the student with the ball begins to dribble around the perimeter of the court while the other players run around the court. When they reach their "home" spot all do a specified number of push-ups, crunches, or curl-ups and begin the passing routine again.

Modifications:

Have students pass the ball overhead to the person behind as they are running. Stress control and cooperation in passing and catching. Challenge the students to see if they can complete two laps without dropping the ball.

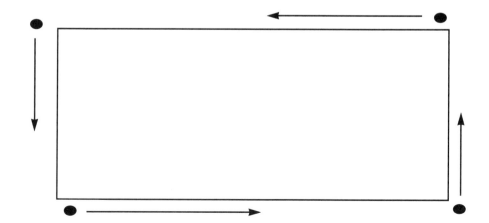

ACTIVITY: DRIBBLE TAG

Focus/ Knowledge Skill	Equipment Needed	Suggested Grade Levels
Refinement of dribbling skills; agility and back defensive skills	1 basketball or other ball for every 2 students (If you do not have enough basketballs, use any ball that will bounce.)	Grades 4–8

Success Notes Remind students to use both the right and left hands, keeping their bodies between the ball and the "tagger."

MAKING IT WORK

Divide the class into two groups. Give each student in one of the groups a ball. On the "go" signal, students begin dribbling while the other students try to tag them on the shoulder. If a player is tagged, loses control of the ball, or stops dribbling, she or he must go to the sideline, and stand and dribble 10 times before returning to the game. After approximately 1 minute, have the students switch roles.

Modification:

Use flag football flags or wrist flags rather than having students tag one another. A student who has a flag pulled is considered tagged.

59

ACTIVITY: END-LINE BASKETBALL

Focus/ Knowledge Skill	Equipment Needed	Suggested Grade Levels
Passing, catching, and defensive skills put into use in a game situation that can relate to most team activities	1 basketball per court Colored vests (pinnies) for half the class	Grades 4–6

Success Notes Remind students to keep in open spaces around the court, and not to crowd around the person with the ball.

MAKING IT WORK

Using as many half-court playing areas as available, and divide the class into groups, assigning two groups to each playing area. The object of this activity is to pass the ball from one person to another without losing possession. The ball is passed in-bounds at one end line. The player with the ball cannot move but must pass the ball to an open teammate. A point is scored when the ball is passed to a teammate over the end line of the opposing team. If the ball is intercepted by the defense, they begin to move the ball toward their opponents' end line.

Modifications:

Using the entire basketball court, divide the class into two groups instead of smaller groups.

```
        0                        0
        X                        X
0              0                      X
goal           X                      goal
        0                        0
        X                        X
```

ACTIVITY: PASS BALL

Focus/ Knowledge Skill	Equipment Needed	Suggested Grade Levels
Throwing, catching, and defensive skills put into use in a game situation that can relate to most team activities	1 Nerf™ soccer ball 2 basketball hoops 2 hula hoops Colored pinnies for half the class	Grades 4–6 Modifications for grade levels: Use adjustable basket heights, with grade 4 students playing on an 8-foot hoop, grade 5 on a 9-foot hoop, and grade 6 on a 10-foot hoop.

Success Notes Hula hoops are hanging from the basketball rims and are used as the goal. This is an excellent activity to develop the concepts of teamwork. Stress the concept of staying spread out and passing to an open teammate.

MAKING IT WORK

Divide the class into two groups and have them stand on opposite sides of the gym. Groups of four or five players from each side come to the center of the floor to begin play. The ball is put into play either by a jump ball or by giving it to one team.

Players cannot dribble or travel with the ball; they may only pass to another teammate or attempt to score. A defensive player may not steal the ball from an opponent but may block or intercept a pass or shot. A team loses possession if the ball is intercepted, a goal is scored, or the ball hits the floor. Fouls are the same as in a basketball game. If a foul occurs, a free shot is given from the foul line.

A player may score in any of four ways:

- 1 point when a ball is thrown through the hula hoop
- 2 points if the ball passes through the regular basketball hoop
- 3 points if the ball passes through either the hula hoop or basketball hoop when shot from behind the top of the basketball key
- 4 points if a shot is made using either a volleyball set or spike, or is caught by a teammate after passing through the hula hoop

ACTIVITY: SMART SHOT

Focus/ Knowledge Skill	Equipment Needed	Suggested Grade Levels
Basketball shooting and offensive strategies.	1 or 2 basketballs for each basket used Cone or poly-spot markers with numbers attached (1 through 3)	Grades 4–8 Modifications for grade levels: Use adjustable basket heights, with grade 4 students playing on an 8-foot hoop, grade 5 on a 9-foot hoop, and grade 6 on a 10-foot hoop. Vary the location of the spots to provide realistic shot-selection distances for skill level of class.

Success Notes Encourage students to select high-percentage shots. Vary the location of the "shot spots" during the activity to provide a continuous challenge and variations depending on ability levels.

MAKING IT WORK

Arrange cones or poly-spot markers on the floor at various shooting distances from each basket to be used. Assign a point value to each spot—3 points for shots close to the basket, 2 points a little farther out, and 1 point for above the key. Attach a card to each cone indicating the point value of a shot made from that location.

Divide students into groups of five and assign to a basket. In relay style, the first player shoots from any location, gets the rebound, and passes to the next player, who takes the shot. This rotation continues for 1 minute. At the end of the time, the points are totaled. Ask teams who scored a high number what shot location the majority of their points came from. Discuss the strategy of taking more high-percentage shots than low-percentage, lucky shots.

Modifications:

Rather than setting a time for each round, have the round stop when one team or all teams reach 40 points.

ACTIVITY: TEAM 21

Focus/ Knowledge Skill	Equipment Needed	Suggested Grade Levels
Shooting and rebounding skills.	2 basketballs per basket 2 cones or poly-spots at each basket	Grades 4–6 Modifications for grade levels: Use adjustable basket heights, with grade 4 students playing on an 8-foot hoop, grade 5 on a 9-foot hoop, and grade 6 on a 10-foot hoop.

Success Notes Allow students to take their long shot from a position on the court that will allow each individual a fair chance to make the basket. Individual variations in location not only will allow for greater personal success but will allow all groups to compete on an equal basis.

MAKING IT WORK

Divide students into equal groups, and ask two groups to go to each basket, forming a line behind a cone or poly-spot marker. On the "go" signal, the first player from each team takes a long shot from a specific distance from the basket. If it is made, the team gets 2 points. The shooter gets the rebound (even if the shot is made) and takes a follow-up shot from the spot closest to where the ball was recovered. If it is made, the team gets 1 point. The first team to get 21 points wins.

Modifications:

- To allow for greater success and to provide skill development for lay-ins, have students dribble toward the basket for the second shot and do a lay-in.
- Individual players can continue to shoot as long as every shot is made. This means that if both the long and short shots are made, the shooter goes back to the long shot for the third attempt. All shots made count, and the shooter continues until a miss or 21 points are scored.

ACTIVITY: BASKETBALL SHUTTLE

Focus/ Knowledge Skill	Equipment Needed	Suggested Grade Levels
Offensive skills of dribbling and shooting are combined with defensive skills and agility.	1 basketball for every 2 students 1 basket at each end of the playing area	Grades 4–8 Modifications for grade levels: Use adjustable basket heights, with grade 4 students playing on an 8-foot hoop, grade 5 on a 9-foot hoop, and grade 6 on a 10-foot hoop.

Success Notes This is a great activity to be used as either a warm-up or a closing game. To increase the success rate for all students, pairings should be rotated every two games; all students move to their right one space, with the end crossing over to the opposite line.

MAKING IT WORK

Place one basketball for every two students on the center line of the basketball court. Divide class into two groups—each lined up on opposite sides of a ball. Have students move back to the end line on their side, staying opposite their partners. On the "go" signal, students run to the center line, touch it with a foot, run back to their end line, and back to the center. The first one back to the center picks up the ball, begins to dribble toward the basket on their side, and attempts a shot. The partner then becomes a defensive player trying to prevent the basket from being made.

If the ball is stolen, tapped away, or shot, the partners place the ball back on the center line. If a shot is made, 1 point is awarded to the shooting team.

Regular rules of basketball apply: double dribble, traveling, and defensive violations.

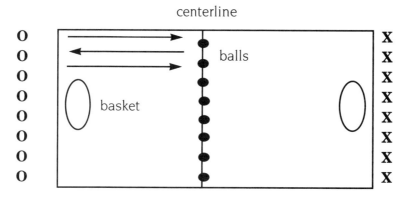

ACTIVITY: BASKETBALL ACTIVITIES FOR SPECIAL NEEDS STUDENTS

Focus/ Knowledge Skill	Equipment Needed	Suggested Grade Levels
Eye-hand coordination skills through basketball skills of passing, catching, shooting, and dribbling in a cooperative format	Basketballs in various sizes, volleyball trainers, yarn balls, playground balls Hula hoops, scooters, target hoops (4',6',8'), wall targets (with letters, numbers, shapes, colors) All equipment should vary in size and color.	Grades 4–8

Success Notes A variety of experiences should be provided, with enough repetition at each developmental level. Using student buddies working as partners, or having special needs students working as a part of a small group, provides reinforcement of learned skills and a "safety net" for students.

MAKING IT WORK

Note: Providing developmentally appropriate activities for students will depend on their individual needs. Care must be taken to determine the appropriate activities and instructional formats that best meet individual abilities and needs. The following activities have been effective.

Instructional Progression

Using a ball appropriate for the student, begin passing the ball between students from a close distance. This progression begins with soft underhand tossing followed by bounce passes and alternating between underhand and bounce passing.

After completing the above progression, begin with a chest pass and overhead pass followed by an alternating pattern.

To begin practicing shooting, have students toss a ball at a wall target from varying distances. As the student experiences success, raise the target, allowing for an arc to be put on the ball when tossed. Hanging a hoop over a basket and asking the student to shoot at the hoop from various distances follows this activity.

Games and Drills
General Modifications:
1. Arrange the court with either a wall target or a hula hoop hanging from a basket. Special needs students can score by hitting the target or shooting the ball through the hoop.

65

2. Wheelchair-bound students get to hold the ball during two "pushes," then must dribble one time.

3. Have students with limited mobility play in a large circle located near the center of the court. When the ball comes into the circle, no other player can go in, reach in, or take the ball away.

4. Use "target hoops" of varying heights in combination with the "circle" concept. Place a target hoop inside the large circle, allowing the student getting the ball to have an opportunity to score by shooting the ball into that hoop.

Successful Games

1. **Scooter Basketball**—Basketball played while sitting on a scooter, using either a small (4´) target hoop or a garbage can on a small table or a mat as the basket. Students in wheelchairs do an excellent job playing this game.

half court

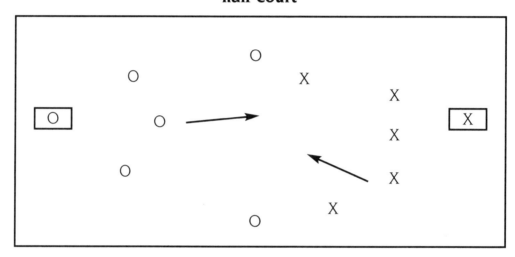

2. **Sideline Basketball**—Half of the students line up on each side of the basketball court. Two or three students from each side come onto the court and begin play. When playing, they may pass to their line players. Line players may only pass down the line or back to the court; they may not score points.

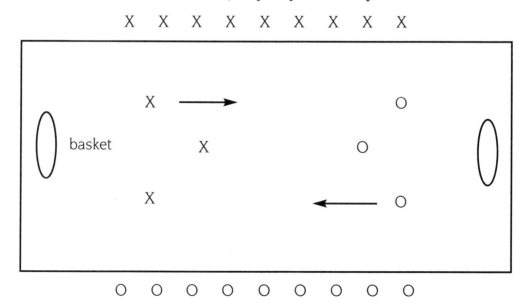

Floor Hockey

- Information for You—Study Guide for Floor Hockey
- Hockey Skill Drills
- Hockey Warm-up
- Beat the Clock
- Hockey Bandits
- Hockey Knockdown
- Keep the Puck
- Straight-Shot Hockey
- One-on-One Hockey
- Four-Goal—Short-Court Hockey
- Hockey Shuttle
- Floor Hockey Activities for Special Needs Students

Information for You

STUDY GUIDE FOR FLOOR HOCKEY

HISTORY

Floor hockey is a modification of ice hockey; it is played in a gym using plastic sticks and either a plastic puck or a ball. There are several differences in the two games, including the marking on the "rink." Ice hockey rinks include a center line, center circle, zone markings, face-off circles, and goal creases. Floor hockey makes use of the center line, center circle, and an enlarged goal crease.

Both games are played with six players on a team: goalkeeper, right and left defense, center, and right and left wings

PLAY

The game begins with a face-off between opposing centers in the center circle. Players then begin dribbling and passing the puck/ball attempting to move into position for a shot. If a shot is made, opposing centers again face-off. Players may move to any position around the "rink" except in the goal crease. A foul is called on any player entering the goal crease.

Several modifications can be used to create greater opportunities for all positions to play an active part. The most important modification to remember is that only the centers may cross the center line; all other players must stay on their side of the rink.

FOULS

Safety is a major concern in floor hockey. Therefore, many of the rules differ from those for ice hockey.

If a player commits a major foul, that player must go to the penalty box for 1 minute for the first major foul, and 2 minutes for the second. On the third, the player is out for the period. A free shot from the 15-foot line is also awarded.

Major fouls include:

1. High-sticking—anytime the blade of the stick comes above the knee
2. Roughing—body checks, tripping, pushing, or other rough play

A player who commits a minor foul receives one warning for the first violation, then 1 minute in the penalty box for each subsequent violation. No free shots are awarded.

Minor fouls include:

1. Crossing the center line
2. Entering the goal crease, with body or stick reaching in
3. Kicking the puck/ball

SCORING

One point is awarded for each shot that crosses the goal line and enters the goal net. Shots may be attempted only from outside the goal crease. The goalkeeper may go out of the goal area but may not use hands or feet to block a shot unless inside the goal crease.

| Fitness Activities | Skill Development | Games That Teach | Healthy Lifestyles | Keeping Track |

ACTIVITY: HOCKEY SKILL DRILLS

Focus/ Knowledge Skill	Equipment Needed	Suggested Grade Levels
Hockey skills of puck/ball control, passing, shooting, and defense are practiced in a fun and challenging format.	1 hockey puck or ball for every 2 students 1 hockey stick for every student Cone markers, wall targets	Grades 4–8 Modifications for grade levels: A soft puck should be used for younger students; a whiffle ball provides a fast game for more skilled classes.

Success Notes Keeping activities safe will increase motivation and fun. Reinforce proper stick control at all times. Anytime the blade comes above the waist—knee for younger students—it is high-sticking and the student should sit out for 1 or 2 minutes.

MAKING IT WORK

Puck and Stick Control

Weave Dribble: Students, in pairs, stand behind a line facing a row of six cones 4–6 feet apart. On the "go" signal, the first player dribbles the puck through the cones, around the end cone, and back through the cones in the opposite direction.

Minefield: Place cone markers, hula hoops, jump ropes, and any other objects randomly around the gym. In pairs, students stand to the outside of the playing area. On the "go" signal, the first student begins to move the puck/ball around the area without hitting any object. On the "stop" signal, the partner runs through the obstacles, takes the stick and puck, and begins to move through the area, while the partner returns to the sideline.

Passing Skills

Target Pass: Partners stand side-by-side, 5 feet apart and 10 feet from a wall. One player hits a whiffle ball into the wall at a 45-degree angle. The second partner receives the ball and returns it to the wall to be received by the other partner.

Pass and Move: Partners stand side-by-side, and one partner has the puck. On the "go" signal, the first partner passes the puck to the other, then moves down the court to receive a pass from the partner.

	Alternating passing and receiving, the group moves randomly around the playing area.
Double Pass:	In-groups of three, with two pucks, stand in a triangle formation. Two of the three players have a puck. On the start signal, those with the puck pass to another partner, who traps it, and passes to another partner.

Shooting Skills

Target Shot:	Mark out a 4′ × 3′ area on a wall. Divide the class into groups equal to the number of playing areas. Each group should have two sticks and one puck. On the "go" signal, the first player in each group dribbles toward the target, and when 10 feet away, takes a shot, retrieves the puck, returns it to the next player, and goes to the end of the line. Shots should be taken from various angles and distances during this drill.
Pass and Shoot:	Using the same format as in Target Shot, the first two players in each line begin by passing the puck between them as they move toward the target. When within 10 feet one partner takes a shot, retrieves the puck, and passes to the other partner, who shoots. After the second shot, the puck is returned to the next pair.

ACTIVITY: HOCKEY WARM-UP

Focus/ Knowledge Skill	Equipment Needed	Suggested Grade Levels
Refine skills related to puck and stick control	1 stick and puck or ball for every two students	Grades 4–6 Modifications for grade levels: For younger students or those less skilled use a juggling cube or milk carton rather than a puck or ball. As students progress, move to a puck or a ball.

Success Notes These activities are designed to review puck and stick control in a challenging and active format. Students should be kept active during the entire time.

MAKING IT WORK

Toss and Dribble: Partners stand approximately 10 feet apart—one with the stick, and the other with the puck. The puck is pushed toward the partner with the stick, who stops it and begins to dribble toward the other partner. When reaching the partner, the dribbler stops, picks up the puck, hands the stick to the partner, and runs back to the starting point to push the puck toward the first partner.

Self Pass: One partner stands with feet approximately shoulder width apart. On signal, the other partner begins dribbling toward the first partner, passes the puck between the feet, quickly moves around, and stops the puck within one stick's length of the partner. Partners then switch places and repeat the activity.

Accuracy Pass: Partners stand approximately 10 feet apart. One partner places heels together and toes wide apart. The other attempts to pass (not shoot) the puck into the open area created by the partner's feet. After three passes from the left and three from the right, partners switch positions.

Circle Relay: Students— in groups of two—are lined up on one side of the facility in relay formation. In front of each group, place a cone approximately 20 feet away and a puck and stick an additional 20 feet away. On the start signal, the first group member runs across, picks up the stick, dribbles the puck to the center, makes a complete circle of the cone, and continues to dribble to the next in line. The second player then reverses the pattern—dribbles to the cone, circles it, continues the dribble to the opposite side, stops the puck, leaves it and the stick there, and returns to the line. This rotation continues for the duration of the activity.

ACTIVITY: BEAT THE CLOCK

Focus/ Knowledge Skill	Equipment Needed	Suggested Grade Levels
Basic hockey skills of passing and receiving are combined in a fast-moving and challenging group activity	1 stick for each player and 1 puck or ball for each group of 10 players	Grades 4–8 Modifications for grade levels: Use a soft, safe puck with younger or less-skilled groups.

Success Notes Begin with each group passing around the circle prior to developing into the fast-moving rotation game.

MAKING IT WORK

The object of this activity is for each group to successfully pass the puck around the circle as quickly as possible.

Divide the class into groups of ten and assign each to a playing area. Students stand in a circle formation approximately 5 feet apart, one player from the group stands in the center, with the puck.

To begin, the center player passes the puck to a player on the circle, who traps it and passes it back to the center. The center then passes to the next player to the right. After the puck has been passed to each player in the circle, the center player exchanges places with a circle player. The rotation continues until all players have been in the center.

Note: After developing appropriate skill levels, this activity can be an excellent opportunity for students to test their skills against the clock or one another. Time each group to see how long it takes to move all players through the rotation. This can also be used as an opportunity to practice the group goal setting process.

Fitness Activities	Skill Development	Games That Teach	Healthy Lifestyles	Keeping Track

ACTIVITY: HOCKEY BANDITS

Focus/ Knowledge Skill	Equipment Needed	Suggested Grade Levels
Dribbling, control of the puck, and defensive skills, combined with various fitness-related activities	1 hockey stick for each player 1 puck or ball for all but 5 students	Grades 4–8

Success Notes Safety must always be stressed. Students called for high-sticking or roughing should receive a penalty of 1–2 minutes out of the game.

MAKING IT WORK

Have students spaced randomly around the facility—each with a hockey stick. Select five students to be "bandits;" these students do not have a puck. On the "go" signal, students begin to dribble the puck anywhere within the playing area. At the same time, the "bandits" move around trying to steal a puck. A player who has the puck stolen becomes a bandit.

After 20–30 seconds, give a "stop" signal. All students begin doing a selected exercise; for example, push-ups, crunches, or treadmills for 1 minute. At the same time, any student without a puck must lay down her or his stick and run 1 lap of the facility, return to the stick and begin doing the exercise for the remaining time.

When the exercise activity has been completed, the "go" signal is given, and play resumes.

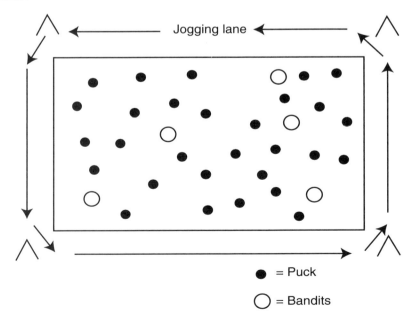

Jogging lane

● = Puck

○ = Bandits

ACTIVITY: HOCKEY KNOCKDOWN

Focus/ Knowledge Skill	Equipment Needed	Suggested Grade Levels
Basic hockey skills of dribbling and passing, combined with defensive skills of stealing. Offensive and defensive transition skills are also stressed.	1 cone marker for each student 5 hockey pucks or balls and 10 hockey sticks for each group of 5 players	Grades 4–7

Success Notes This is a great activity that keeps students active and stresses the use of puck or ball and stick control. Stress the control aspects of the activity by making sure that shots are taken only from the marked sideline.

MAKING IT WORK

Students are divided into two groups—each assigned to one side of the gym. Each student should be given one cone marker to place approximately 3 feet behind his or her position on the sideline. Hockey sticks and pucks are placed in the center of the playing area. Players on each side should be given a number 1 through 5. When a player's number is called, that player runs to the center, picks up a stick, and begins playing a puck.

Players attempt to dribble the puck toward their opponents' "free" cone, and hit the cone by shooting from the marked sideline. After a shot has been attempted by each pairing, pucks and sticks are taken back to the center, players take their positions on the sideline, and another number is called.

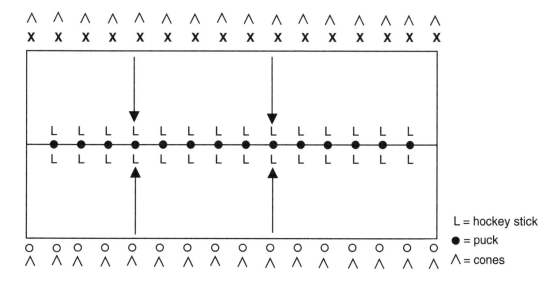

L = hockey stick
● = puck
∧ = cones

ACTIVITY: KEEP THE PUCK

Focus/ Knowledge Skill	Equipment Needed	Suggested Grade Levels
Hockey skills of puck control, passing, defense, and team play are used in this challenging game.	1 hockey stick for each player 1 ball or puck for each game Colored jerseys for one team	Grades 6–8 Modifications for grade levels: Have the teams consist of almost equal numbers

Success Notes This activity is challenging for the groups with fewer players. If they retain the puck for the entire game, award them with extra points.

MAKING IT WORK

Divide the class into two equal teams—one wearing the colored jerseys. To begin the game, six players from one team come to the court and ten from the other. On the "go" signal, play begins. The object is for the team with the fewer players to pass and dribble, keeping the puck until time is called—1 or 2 minutes.

The defensive team is awarded 1 point for each steal (they must have control). The offensive team is awarded 4 points if they keep possession for the entire time.

After time is called, players return to their sideline and a new group comes to the floor. At each rotation, teams switch roles; the offensive team becomes defensive—more players—and the defensive team becomes offensive—fewer players.

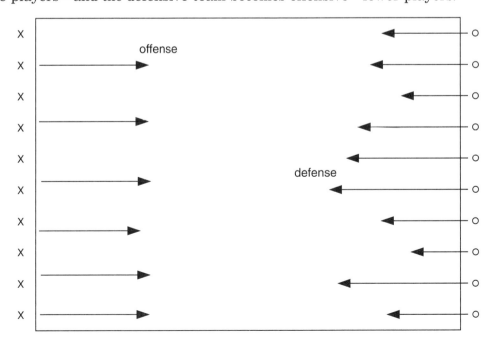

ACTIVITY: STRAIGHT SHOT HOCKEY

Focus/ Knowledge Skill	Equipment Needed	Suggested Grade Levels
Practice the hockey skills of dribbling, shooting, defense, and goal keeping.	1 floor hockey stick for each student and 15 hockey pucks or balls 22 plastic bowling pins or liter pop bottles	Grades 4–7 Modifications for grade levels: Students in grades 4–5 should be placed in smaller groupings to allow for more play.

Success Notes This is an excellent activity to keep all students active and involved. Place target areas that will allow for the best chance of being hit by a good shot.

MAKING IT WORK

Divide students into two groups. Assign one group to each side of the playing area. Place five plastic bowling pins behind each end line and six along each side (three on each half of the area). Half of the players from each team are offense, and the others play defense.

On the "go" signal, offensive players from each team begin to dribble their pucks past defending players to hit a bowling pin. Once a pin is hit, it is out of play for the remainder of the game. Teams receive 1 point for each pin they knock over. The game should last for approximately 3 minutes or until all pins have been knocked over.

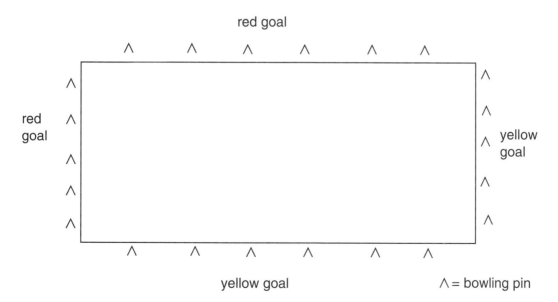

ACTIVITY: ONE-ON-ONE HOCKEY

Focus/ Knowledge Skill	Equipment Needed	Suggested Grade Levels
Hockey skills of stick control, dribbling, and defense	4 cones or markers for each playing area 2 hockey sticks and one puck or ball for each playing area	Grades 4–8

Success Notes Stress control and dribbling. Students should be discouraged from taking long and uncontrolled shots. The objective is to move past a defender and control the puck to the goal.

MAKING IT WORK

Set up several playing areas across the gym. Each playing area should be approximately 40 feet long by 20 feet wide. At each end, set a goal area marked by cones or other markers.

Have students get in equal groups behind each goal area. Each group should have one stick. A puck should be given to one group at each area. On the "go" signal, play begins at all areas. The first player on each side attempts to score by dribbling and shooting the puck past the opponents' goal. When a goal is scored, the ball passes the end line, or it goes out-of-bounds, play stops. Players go back to their lines and the next two players come out and begin.

Using this format, each playing area will be starting and finishing individual games at different times.

| Fitness Activities | Skill Development | Games That Teach | Healthy Lifestyles | Keeping Track |

ACTIVITY: FOUR-GOAL—SHORT-COURT HOCKEY

Focus/ Knowledge Skill	Equipment Needed	Suggested Grade Levels
Refinement of hockey skills and team play in a game situation.	12 hockey sticks (6 red and 6 yellow) and one puck or ball for each court 8 cones or poly-spot markers for each court (place a piece of red paper on the red goals and yellow on the yellow goals).	Grades 4–8 Modifications for grade levels: Grade 4: Have only 5 players per side. This gives a greater opportunity to pass and is less confusing.

Success Notes Keep the game moving quickly while stressing passing and strategy. Have students monitor and be responsible for their own games (calling fouls, bringing the puck to the center, and starting the play). If only one game is played at a time, rotate players in every minute.

MAKING IT WORK

Using half of a basketball court, place one goal on each side and one at each end. Designate two of the goals to be red and two yellow. Assign six players to the "red" team and six to the "yellow" team. Have one player from each team stand near each goal area, with the other players toward the center. Tell students that they may move anywhere on the court, but if they stay in the general area assigned, it keeps the action spread out and provides for a better game; there are no goalies. To begin the game, the puck is placed between two opposing players. On the "go signal," play begins. A score is made when the puck is hit past the goal area. Red shoots through the red goals and yellow through the yellow goals. When a goal is scored, players return to their positions and the puck is again dropped in the center.

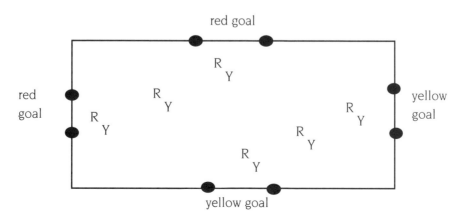

ACTIVITY: HOCKEY SHUTTLE

Focus/ Knowledge Skill	Equipment Needed	Suggested Grade Levels
Offensive skills of puck control and shooting are combined with defensive skills and agility.	2 hockey sticks and 1 puck or ball for every 2 students	Grades 4–8

Success Notes This activity keeps all students active and can be used as a warm-up or skill-development drill. To increase the success rate for all students, pairings should be rotated every two or three games; all students move to their right one space, with the ends crossing over to the opposite line.

MAKING IT WORK

Place one hockey puck for every two students on the center line of the playing area. Place one hockey stick on each side of the puck. Divide the class into two groups, lined up on opposite sides of a puck. Have students move back to the end line on their side, staying opposite their partners. On the "go" signal, students run to the center line, touch it with a foot, run back to the end line and back to the center, and pick up their sticks. The first player of each pair to begin playing the puck is on offense; the other is on defense. The offensive player attempts to dribble the ball back past the defender's end line. The defensive player tries to steal the puck and control it.

Play stops if the defensive player gains control or the offensive player maintains control while crossing the end line, scoring a point for their team. If a foul occurs (roughing, etc.), a point is awarded to the nonfouling team.

Note: If sides are not equal one group plays 2 on 1.

● = puck
L = hockey stick

ACTIVITY: FLOOR HOCKEY ACTIVITIES FOR SPECIAL NEEDS STUDENTS

Focus/ Knowledge Skill	Equipment Needed	Suggested Grade Levels
Eye-hand coordination, agility, basic coordination, and team skills taught through passing, shooting, and dribbling activities	Pint milk cartons, Nerf™ soccer balls, foam balls, hockey sticks, Pillow-Polo® sticks, soft hockey pucks All equipment in various sizes and colors	Grades 4–8

Success Notes A variety of experiences should be provided, with enough repetition at each developmental level. Using student buddies working as partners, or having special needs students working as a part of a small group, provides reinforcement of learned skills and a "safety net" for students.

MAKING IT WORK

Note: Providing developmentally appropriate activities for students will depend on their individual needs. Care must be taken to determine the appropriate activities and instructional formats that best meet individual abilities and needs. The following activities have been shown to be effective.

Instructional Progression

The basic skills of floor hockey are very similar to those in soccer. When participating in floor hockey, students must be cautioned and reminded to keep the blade of the stick below the knees at all times.

Beginning with milk cartons, have students move them around the gym with the hockey sticks. After basic control has been achieved, students should pass back and forth to their buddy—first from a stationary position, progressing to moving at slow speed. Try progressing from milk cartons to Nerf™ soccer balls, and finally, to soft hockey pucks.

To practice shooting, begin from a short distance, hitting the object between two cone markers approximately six feet apart. Progress to dribbling toward the goal and shooting at a wall target or goal.

Games and Drills

Special needs students can successfully participate in most lead-up and regular floor hockey games with some simple modifications.

81

Scooter Floor Hockey: Use plastic hockey sticks that have had the handles cut to approximately 6 inches in length above the blade (students in wheelchairs may use a regular-length stick). All students sit on scooters, or in wheelchairs, and play a regulation game of floor hockey.

General Modifications:

Have the special needs student play inside a large circle in front of the goal or at one side of the court. If the puck is hit into this area, only the student in the area may hit the ball. This is a good time to use a buddy—having both students stand in the circle, with the special needs student hitting the ball while the buddy traps and passes.

Students with limited mobility or agility can be used as goalies, with a slightly smaller goal area. **Note:** Make a goal box of approximately 10′ × 10′ in front of the goal. No other players may enter, or have their sticks enter, the goal area.

Try using a larger ball—a Nerf™ soccer ball, 5 1/2-inch playground ball, foam ball, or milk cartons.

Soccer

Information for You

STUDY GUIDE FOR SOCCER

HISTORY

The Romans, who learned it from the Greeks, played one of the first known forms of soccer. Over the years, the game changed. Soccer as we know it today was played in English villages during the tenth century. Today, people of all ages play in over 120 countries throughout the world. The first regulation game to be played in America took place in 1869. Soccer, or football as it is called in all countries except the United States and Canada, is the most widely played sport in the world.

BENEFITS

Soccer can be adapted and played almost anywhere by diverse groups of people. Little equipment is necessary and it is inexpensive. Soccer is an excellent cardiovascular activity that has simple and easy-to-understand rules.

RULES

- The official game is played with 11 players on each side.

- Prior to the kickoff, the offensive team must be behind the center line, while the defensive team remains 10 yards from the ball on their side.

- Each goal is counted as 1 point and is scored when the ball goes over the goal line between the goals. After a score, the ball goes back to the midline, and the team that was scored on gets the ball for the kickoff.

- There are two kinds of free kicks—direct and indirect. A direct free kick is a kick that may be scored directly without touching another player. Direct kicks are awarded to a team when the opponents commit one of the following fouls—push, trip, hold, or kick an opponent.

- Indirect kicks cannot score directly; they must first be touched by another player. Indirect kicks are awarded to a team when the opponent commits one of the following fouls—touching the ball with hands or arms, kicking the ball backward on a penalty kick, offside, interfering with the goalie, the goalie carrying the ball more than four steps, or unsportsmanlike conduct. For either direct or indirect kicks, defenders must be at least 10 yards away from the ball.

- During a direct penalty kick, the ball is placed on the penalty spot and only the kicker and goal are involved in play.

- When doing a throw-in, both of the players' feet must remain on the ground. The player must face the direction of the throw and throw the ball from over the top of his or her head.

- A "goal kick" is awarded to the defending team if an offensive player kicks the ball out of bounds across the goal line.

- A "corner kick" is awarded when the ball crosses over the goal line and is last touched by a defensive player. A goal may be scored directly from a corner kick.

- Team positions are:

  Goalie: Goalies may stop the ball from passing into the goal and may use their hands and feet. When holding the ball, they may take only four steps towards midfield. They may clear the ball with a kick, or throw with one or two hands.

  Backs: Backs stay in the backfield to help the goalie defend the goal.

  Centers: Centers play front and back; they score goals as well as defend their goal.

  Forwards: Forwards stay in the front part of the field and assist in scoring.

ACTIVITY: SOCCER SKILL DRILLS

Focus/ Knowledge Skill	Equipment Needed	Suggested Grade Levels
Soccer skills, including footwork, dribbling, trapping, passing, and kicking, are presented through fun and challenging activities	1 soccer ball for every 2 players Cone markers, hula hoops, wall targets, poly-spots	Grades 4–8 Modifications for grade levels: Younger students and those with less skill should use Nerf™ or low pressure soccer balls.

Success Notes These activities present a challenge for students. As they move through the progressions, add challenges designed for skill levels of individual students. This helps to ensure continued learning and motivation.

MAKING IT WORK

Ball Control Drills

Random Dribbling: Students are in pairs. One student takes the ball and begins to dribble around the play area, keeping the ball close enough to trap it within one step when the "stop" signal is given. On the "stop" signal, the partner without the ball runs to the first partner, takes the ball, and begins to dribble, while the other partner does jumping jacks. This rotation continues until all players have had several attempts.

Dribble Chase: In pairs, one student begins to dribble the ball around the play area, changing directions and speed randomly. The partner without the ball follows, trying to copy the movements. On the "switch" signal, partners change positions.

Obstacle Dribble: Place hula hoops, cones, and other safe objects around the play area. On the "go" signal, students with a ball begin to dribble around the area, avoiding the obstacles. On the "change" signal, the second partner runs to the first partner, takes the ball, and begins to dribble, while the first person to dribble returns to the sideline.

Pass and Run: Place six poly-spots or cone markers in a circle formation (15–20 feet in diameter), and assign one student to each place, forming a circle facing inward. To begin, one student passes the ball to another player not standing next to her or him. After passing, the first player follows the pass and takes the position of the receiving player, who will be passing to another player. **Note:** This activity can become confusing. Make sure students understand that they follow the pass and don't interfere with any pass being made.

Trapping Drills

Wall Trap: Standing approximately 10 feet from a wall, toss the ball into the wall and trap the rebound after it has bounced. Use different parts of the foot and leg to trap with. After they are successful with tossing and trapping, allow students to kick the ball into the wall.

Partner Trap: Standing approximately 5–8 feet from a partner, alternate tossing the ball lightly toward your partner. Toss it at the legs, feet, and chest. Once the ball is controlled, reverse roles.

Kicking, Passing, and Shooting Drills

Triangle Kick: Three players form a triangle, standing approximately 10 feet apart, each group with two balls. Beginning from one lower corner of the triangle, the player passes the ball to the "top" person who passes it back. As soon as the ball is passed back, the other person passes to the top player. After 10 passes to the top player, everyone rotates one position to the right.

Hoop Target: In groups of three with one ball and one hoop, players form a line, with players 10 feet away from one another. The center person holds the hoop to the side, and one of the end players passes the ball through the hoop to the other end player. After passing, the players exchange positions with the center player. This rotation continues until each player has made 15 successful kicks.

Goal Kicks: In groups of two—each with a ball and standing by two cones 8 feet apart—one player stands 20 feet away from the cones while the other stands behind them. The player with the ball begins to dribble toward the cones, and when approximately 10 feet away, takes a shot. The player behind the goal retrieves the ball and dribbles to the start line, the shooting partner takes the position behind the goal. Note: Narrow the goal to form a greater challenge, and have players shoot from different angles.

ACTIVITY: ADD-A-BALL SOCCER

Focus/ Knowledge Skill	Equipment Needed	Suggested Grade Levels
Offensive skills of soccer, including passing, dribbling, receiving, trapping Defensive skills of soccer, including guarding, stealing Cooperation and agility are also stressed.	2 Nerf™ or regular soccer balls Cone markers Colored vests (pinnies)	Grades 5–8

Success Notes Use two different-colored balls so students can easily tell which is the "new ball." When adding the "new ball," place it on the floor at least half a court away from where play is taking place.

MAKING IT WORK

Divide the class into two teams in different-colored pinnies—each standing on one side of the playing area. The first three players from each team come to the center, spacing themselves out on the center line (there are no goalies). To begin, place the ball between two players and say "go." The players begin playing a regular 3-on-3 game. At any point in the game the "new ball" is dropped and the signal "New ball" is given. At that point, players leave the ball they are playing and begin play with the new ball; the "old" ball is picked up. A goal is scored when the ball passes the opponent's end line and is trapped by an offensive player within three feet of the line.

Continue play with this group for $1\frac{1}{2}$–2 minutes, putting a "new ball" in play every 15 seconds. After completing their game, players go to the end of the line, and the next three from each team line up on the center line.

| Fitness Activities | Skill Development | Games That Teach | Healthy Lifestyles | Keeping Track |

ACTIVITY: FOUR-GOAL SOCCER

Focus/ Knowledge Skill	Equipment Needed	Suggested Grade Levels
Dribbling, passing, goalkeeping, and game strategies are emphasized.	4 soccer goals (cones or other markers) Colored pinnies 2 soccer balls	Grades 5–8 Modifications for grade levels: Field size may be modified for younger or less-skilled players. Slightly deflate balls or use Nerf™ soccer balls for younger or less-skilled groups.

Success Notes Stress teamwork through passing and cooperation during this activity. To be successful at this level, students should also learn to play positions or areas.

MAKING IT WORK
Arrange the area to be used in a large square with each sideline approximately 40 to 50 yards in length. A goal area is set in the middle of each sideline and should measure approximately 6 feet in width. Regular soccer rules regarding the use of hands, and body contact, should be stressed. Two soccer balls are in play at all times.

Divide the class into equal teams, with each team defending two goals and having a goalie in each. To begin, one ball is given to a goalie from each team. The goalies put the balls into play with goal kicks. From that point, field play is the same as in regular soccer. When a goal is scored play does not stop, as the other ball is still in play. The ball is put back into play with a goal kick by the goalie scored upon.

Modification:
Use two different-colored balls. Have each team able to score with only one color; for example, the red team may score with only the red ball.

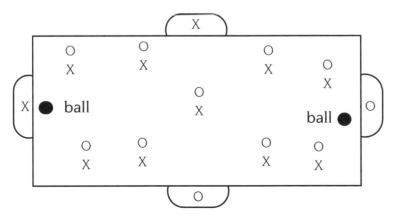

ACTIVITY: SHORT-COURT SOCCER

Focus/ Knowledge Skill	Equipment Needed	Suggested Grade Levels
Offensive skills of dribbling, passing, and shooting defensive skills of guarding, blocking, and stealing	1 soccer ball per playing area 4 cone markers per playing area Colored pinnies as needed	Grades 4–7 Modifications for grade levels: Grades 4–5 should play on fields approximately 30 yards in length and 15–20 yards in width. Grades 6–8 should play on fields approximately 50 yards long and 20–30 yards in width.

Success Notes Stress passing and team involvement at all times. Use cones for goal areas, with the goal approximately 4 feet in width. Play goes much faster and more skills are developed if a goalie is not used.

MAKING IT WORK

This is a fast-paced activity using the concepts and skills of regulation soccer in a modified format.

Divide students into groups of four with two groups assigned to each playing area. To begin, have students pick a partner from the opposite team to guard; students should stay with their partners on both offense and defense. On the "go" signal, one player is given the ball and play begins. Keep technical rules to a minimum and stress movement, proper spacing, accurate passing, and good defensive skills.

To score, the ball must be passed to a player standing inside the area marked as the goal. The receiving player must trap and control the ball within that area to receive 2 points. If the player traps and controls the ball outside the goal area but past the end line, 1 point is awarded. After a goal is scored, the ball is given to the opposite team at midfield.

Modification:

Place the cones forming the goal farther apart, and allow students to score by kicking the ball through the goal.

ACTIVITY: SOCCER GOLF

Focus/ Knowledge Skill	Equipment Needed	Suggested Grade Levels
Development of foot-eye coordination and ball control through dribbling and passing	9 Nerf™ or regular soccer balls 9 hula hoops Nonadhesive marking tape Marking cones and poly-spots Score cards and pencils	Grades 4–8 Modifications in the design of each hole should be made according to ability levels of the students.

Success Notes Each hole should be designed to be both challenging and success-oriented for all students. Depending on the skill of players, add sharp doglegs, hazards, and so on. Stress slow movement and control of the ball. If playing doubles, stress the need for cooperation and accurate passing.

Post scores, give handicaps, have a tournament.

MAKING IT WORK

Individual Play:

Students are placed in groups at each hole—in "shot-gun" start format. To begin play, one player takes a ball and begins dribbling down the hole. A "stroke" is counted each time contact is made with the ball. Play is stopped and the number of strokes counted when the player is inside the hula hoop and traps the ball. A one-stroke penalty is added each time the ball touches a hazard. If the ball goes out-of-bounds one stroke is added and the ball is picked up and placed into play where it went out-of-bounds.

When one player completes the hole, the next player in the group begins. After all players in the group finish the hole the group moves to the next hole.

Partner Play:

Rules and playing format are the same in both individual and partner play. However, in partner play, students are placed in groups of two, with each group having one ball. One partner tees off by passing to the other partner, who must trap the ball. The partner who teed off then runs forward of the receiving partner and receives the next pass. This rotation continues until the ball is trapped inside the hula hoop. Again, one stroke is counted for every pass made. Penalty strokes are added for hitting a hazard or going out-of-bounds.

ACTIVITY: SOCCER SHOOT AND RUN

Focus/ Knowledge Skill	Equipment Needed	Suggested Grade Levels
Soccer skills of dribbling, shooting, and goal keeping; cardiovascular fitness	6 soccer balls 12 cone markers or 6 small goals 30 cones, poly-spots, or other markers	Grades 4–6 Modifications for grade levels: The difficulty of the obstacle course should be changed depending on the ability of students. Keep in mind that they all need to experience success while being challenged.

Success Notes Vary the obstacle course at each area along with the size of the goal. This will increase the difficulty in both controlling the dribble and goal-keeping.

MAKING IT WORK

Set up six playing areas at different locations. At each area, place an obstacle course of cones or other markers, a goal area, and a soccer ball. Divide students into groups and assign each to a different location. Once at the station, one player takes the goalie's position, and the others form a line behind the obstacle course. On the "go" signal, the first person in each line takes the ball, dribbles through the cones, and takes a shot. After taking the shot, the ballhandler trades places with the goalie. The goalie then runs one complete lap around the entire playing area, stops at the goal past the one just played, and joins the shooting line. This rotation is continued until all players have taken shots and played goalie at each station.

Modifications:

Have students go out in groups of two, and pass the ball between them prior to one taking the shot. For the rotation, one person of the pair goes to goal while the other returns to the shooting line. After the second turn in the shooting line, the second person plays goalie.

ACTIVITY: SOCCER WARM-UPS

Focus/ Knowledge Skill	Equipment Needed	Suggested Grade Levels
Refine skills related to ball control. Participate in cooperative activities.	Soccer balls (1 for every 2 students)	Grades 4–8

Success Notes These are quick-moving activities designed to review ball-control skills in a fun and active format. As this portion of the lesson is a review, keep the direct instruction to a minimum. Instead, move around the area and provide feedback to specific individual students. Rotate between the active and passive partner about every 15–20 seconds.

MAKING IT WORK

The following activities are done in pairs, with each pair having a ball.

Toe-Tap Challenge: One partner places the ball directly in front of herself or himself and lightly places one foot on top of it. On the "go" signal, the player begins switching feet, trying to keep the ball still while keeping balance and control of the ball. The other partner begins doing jumping jacks. After 15 seconds, the partners switch activities. This rotation should be repeated two or three times.

Partner Dribble Around: One partner assumes a push-up position, while the other stands ready to begin dribbling the ball. On the start signal, the partner with the ball begins dribbling around the partner who is now doing push-ups. After 15 seconds, the signal to change directions is given. The partner who is dribbling changes directions, and the other keeps doing push-ups. After 30 seconds, partners switch activities.

Self-Pass: One partner stands with feet approximately shoulder-width apart. On signal, the other partner begins dribbling toward the partner. When approximately 2 feet away, the second partner passes the ball between the feet and moves quickly around to trap the ball within 2 feet of the first partner. Partners then switch places and repeat the activity.

Quick-Turn Relay: Students, in groups of two, are lined up on one side of the facility in relay formation. In front of each group place a cone approximately 20 feet away and a soccer ball an additional 20 feet away. On the start signal, the first group member runs across to the ball, dribbles it to the center cone, makes a complete circle of the cone, and continues dribbling to the partner. The second partner reverses the pattern by dribbling to the cone, circling it, and continuing the dribble to the opposite side, traps the ball, leaves it there, and returns to the line. This rotation continues for the duration of the activity.

93

ACTIVITY: PIN BALL

Focus/ Knowledge Skill	Equipment Needed	Suggested Grade Levels
Offensive skills of dribbling and controlled passing or shooting are emphasized, along with defensive skills and agility.	Plastic bowling pins, plastic pop bottles, or cone markers for all but 3–4 students 1 slightly deflated soccer ball, Nerf™ soccer ball, or Gatorskin® ball for each student	Grades 4–8 Modifications for grade levels: Increase or decrease the number of "free rovers" depending on grade level and abilities.

Success Notes Keep the game moving at all times. Encourage students to take a risk and leave their pins to dribble and get someone else.

MAKING IT WORK

The object of this game is to dribble a ball close to another person's pin, kick the ball into the pin, and knock it over. At the same time, players are trying to defend their pins from others.

Assign four to five players the position of "rover." The remaining students should each be given a pin and a ball. Pins should be randomly spaced around the gym, away from walls. On the "go" signal, all students begin moving, trying to maneuver into a position to kick their balls into another player's pin. Rovers may steal a ball, or retrieve any loose ball and kick it into a pin. When a player's pin is knocked over, that player must pick it up and run 1 lap of the gym before replacing the pin in play.

In defending, pin players must not use their hands or place the pin between their feet to keep it from falling when hit. If a violation occurs, the player must run 2 laps of the gym before returning to play.

Safety Note: Use deflated or soft balls, and emphasize to all students that kicks must be controlled. The objective of the game is to perform a controlled kick into a pin from a fairly short distance. If a ball is kicked hard or goes above waist high the person kicking should first be warned. If it happens again, the player should be removed from the game for a period of time.

ACTIVITY: COURTSIDE SOCCER

Focus/ Knowledge Skill	Equipment Needed	Suggested Grade Levels
Basic offensive and defensive soccer skills are used on a short court, requiring quick passing and ball control.	Nerf™ or slightly flat soccer ball Colored pinnies	Grades 4–6 Modifications for grade levels: For more advanced students, two balls may be used at the same time.

Success Notes To keep sideline goalies active have them "scramble" to exchange places after each 30 seconds of play. When the scramble takes place, all sideline goalies must move from an end line position to a sideline position. Play does not stop when the scramble takes place.

MAKING IT WORK
This game utilizes the lines of both volleyball and basketball courts.

Divide students into two groups, with each group assigned to one end of the remaining basketball court. Half of the players from each group come into the volleyball court area, with the remaining players spread out around the end lines and sidelines on their respective sides.

"Active" players—those within the volleyball court lines—dribble, pass, and shoot while the goalies defend their goal lines. Active players must stay within the volleyball court boundaries, and all shots must be taken from within that area. Goalies may move between the basketball end lines and sidelines but may not enter the volleyball court. Kicking the ball, no higher than waist high, past the opponents' line of goalies scores a goal.

Modification:
Add a second ball when players have gained necessary skills.

ACTIVITY: OFFENSE-DEFENSE

Focus/ Knowledge Skill	Equipment Needed	Suggested Grade Levels
All regular soccer skills are included in this fast-moving activity.	1 soccer ball and set of pinnies for each playing area	Grades 5–8

Success Notes Prior to playing this game, students should have the appropriate skills to be successful in passing, dribbling, and team play.

MAKING IT WORK

Divide class into groups of seven, assign two groups to each 25 yd. × 50 yd. playing area.

The object is for the offensive team to move the ball down the floor and score a goal by kicking the ball into the goal area, and for the defensive team to intercept the ball and move it past the center line.

Play begins with the offensive team lined up at their end line and the defense at theirs. The offensive team begins by dribbling and passing down the field. The defense, playing appropriate positions, tries to disrupt play and steal the ball. If the defense takes control of the ball, they attempt to dribble and pass the ball over the center line. To score, the defense must trap and stop the ball within 5 yards of the center line.

If either team scores, play begins again with the offense taking control at their end line.

After 5 minutes of play, offensive and defensive teams switch positions and begin play.

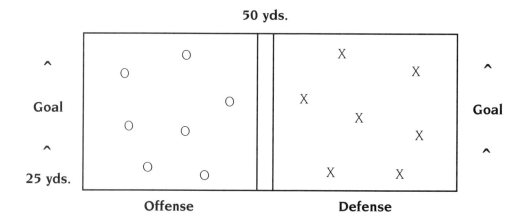

50 yds.

Goal   Goal

25 yds.

Offense   Defense

ACTIVITY: SOCCER GRAB

Focus/ Knowledge Skill	Equipment Needed	Suggested Grade Levels
Basic soccer skills of dribbling and passing, combined with defensive skills of intercepting and transitions from offense to defense.	Nerf™ or slightly deflated soccer ball Colored pinnies for each team Cone markers or poly-spots	Grades 4–8 Modifications for grade levels: As students progress in skill level, divide the class into smaller groups (6 per team).

Success Notes Stress cooperation and teamwork. If students begin to "bunch-up" around the ball divide the court into specific playing areas, having one player from each team assigned to that area.

MAKING IT WORK

The object of this activity is to dribble and pass the ball down the court and pass it to the goal player standing inside the goalie area.

To begin, divide the class into two teams. One player of each team is assigned to be the goal player. Other players move to positions around the court. Play begins in the center by dropping the ball between two opposing players. Players dribble and pass moving the ball toward the goal. When the ball is successfully passed to the goal player, play stops, new goal players are assigned, and play begins with another dropped ball.

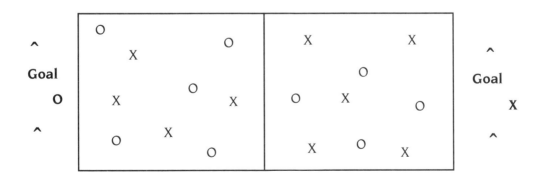

| Fitness Activities | Skill Development | Games That Teach | Healthy Lifestyles | Keeping Track |

ACTIVITY: SOCCER SHUTTLE

Focus/ Knowledge Skill	Equipment Needed	Suggested Grade Levels
Offensive skills of dribbling and shooting are combined with defensive skills and agility.	1 soccer ball for every 2 students 1 soccer goal at each end of the playing area	Grades 4–8 Modifications for grade levels: Adjust the length of the playing area, making it shorter for younger students.

Success Notes This is a great activity to be used as either warm-up or closing game. To increase the success rate for all students, pairings should be rotated every two or three games; all students move to their right one space, with the ends crossing over to the opposite line.

MAKING IT WORK

This activity can be played either inside a gym or outside on a soccer field.

Place one soccer ball for every two students on the center line of the playing area. Divide the class into two groups, lined up on opposite sides of a ball. Have students move back to the end line on their side, staying opposite their partners. On the "go" signal, students run to the center line, touch it with a foot, run back to their end line, and back to the center. The first one back to the center takes control of the ball, begins to dribble toward the goal on their side, and attempts a shot from approximately 10 feet away. When one player gains control of the ball, the other becomes a defensive player trying to steal the ball and prevent the shot from being taken.

If the ball is stolen, tapped away, or shot, the partners place the ball back on the center line. If a shot is made, 1 point is awarded to the shooting team.

Regular rules of soccer apply. If a violation occurs, 1 point is awarded to the nonoffending team.

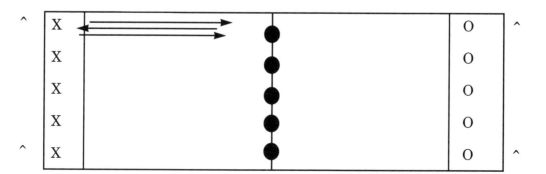

ACTIVITY: LANE SOCCER

Focus/ Knowledge Skill	Equipment Needed	Suggested Grade Levels
Skills of dribbling, passing, tackling, guarding an opponent, and position play are utilized in this activity.	1 soccer ball Cone markers Colored vests	Grades 6–8

Success Notes The purpose of this activity is to enhance passing and position-play skills. To be successful, students must be reminded to pass with accuracy and play their positions.

MAKING IT WORK

To prepare the playing area, mark out a 50 × 75-yard area with 5 ten-foot lanes; lanes can be marked with cone markers, poly-spots, or chalk lines.

The object of the game is for the offensive team to pass the ball down the field and kick it past the opposite end line, and for the defensive team to intercept the ball and dribble it past the center line. Divide the class into two equal teams—one beginning as offense the other as defense. Have players arrange themselves in equal lines behind each lane. When playing, all offensive players must remain in their lanes. Defensive players in lanes 1, 3, and 5 must remain in their lanes, but players in lanes 2 and 4 may move one lane on either side.

To begin, an offensive player begins moving the ball down the field, defensive players leave their end line and move, in their lanes, toward the offensive team. Play continues until a point is scored by either team or 2 minutes have passed. At the conclusion of the game, players rotate to the ends of the line in their lane. After one round, teams switch ends.

Fouls are called as in regulation soccer. However, if the offensive team commits a foul, the game is over. If, the defensive team commits a foul, the ball is given to the offensive team for 1 free pass.

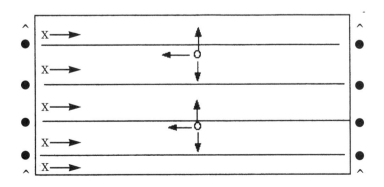

ACTIVITY: ADD-ON SOCCER

Focus/ Knowledge Skill	Equipment Needed	Suggested Grade Levels
All regular soccer skills are included in this fast-moving activity.	1 soccer ball and set of colored vests for each playing area	Grades 7–8

Success Notes Students must be reminded that this is a fast-moving activity requiring that sideline players quickly rotate in at appropriate times.

MAKING IT WORK

Divide class into groups of six, assign two groups to each 25 yd. × 50 yd. playing area. Prior to beginning play, three members of each group take up positions on the field, with the remaining three standing on the sideline.

The object is to move the ball, under control, past the end line of the opposing team. To begin, one team kicks off from the center line. Play continues until a point is scored, a foul is committed, or the ball goes out of bounds. If a foul is committed or the ball goes out-of-bounds, the team not making the mistake adds one player. Players continue to be added in this manner until a goal is scored or all six players from both teams are on the field.

After one game has been completed, a new game begins with the first players from the previous game standing on the sideline.

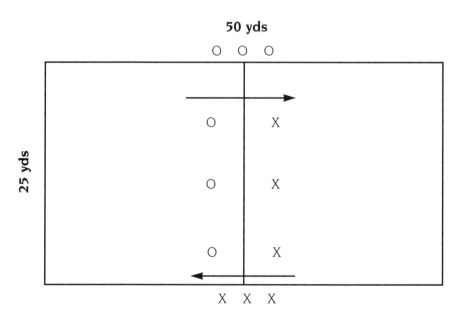

ACTIVITY: SOCCER ACTIVITIES FOR SPECIAL NEEDS STUDENTS

Focus/ Knowledge Skill	Equipment Needed	Suggested Grade Levels
Eye-hand and foot-eye coordination, agility, and team skills are enhanced through soccer skills of passing, dribbling, and trapping.	Nerf™ soccer balls, milk cartons, gym mats, tennis balls, scooters, cone markers, and hockey sticks All equipment should vary in size and color.	Grade 4–8

Success Notes A variety of experiences should be provided with enough repetition at each developmental level. Using student buddies working as partners, or having special needs students working as a part of a small group, provides reinforcement of learned skills and a "safety net" for students.

MAKING IT WORK

Note: Providing developmentally appropriate activities for students will depend on their individual needs. Care must be taken to determine the appropriate activities and instructional formats that best meet individual abilities and needs. The following activities have been proven effective.

Instructional Progression

From a close distance, buddies begin rolling a ball to their partners. Partners stop the ball and return it, using a "soft" kick. If students do not have the use of their legs, they may use a hockey stick to stop and pass the ball.

To teach dribbling skills, begin with milk cartons and progress to juggling cubes followed by balls. Begin by having students move a short distance to a cone, stop, and move to another cone. After they experience success in dribbling short distances, have them try moving around cones, controlling the ball through the movement.

Many special needs students enjoy success while playing goalie, with the assistance of a buddy. Teaching these skills involves eye-hand coordination and agility. Practice these skills by tossing a volleyball trainer or other large, soft ball from various distances and locations. Progress to tossing a slightly deflated soccer ball, followed by kicking the ball to the goalie. When using a buddy, have the assisting student locate the ball and back up the partner.

Games and Drills

Special needs students can successfully participate in most lead-up and regular soccer games with some simple modifications.

101

Clean Up the Gym: This activity can be played either in the gym or on an outdoor field. Arrange students in lines, each behind a hula hoop. At the center line, place a cone marker for each line of students. At the far end of the playing area, place as many balls (soccer, playground, softball, whiffle) as available. On the "go" signal, students—in relay fashion—run to a ball, dribble it to their cone, stop, do 5 jumping jacks, continue to dribble back to their hoop, pick up the ball, and place it in the hoop. Play continues until all balls have been placed in a hula hoop.

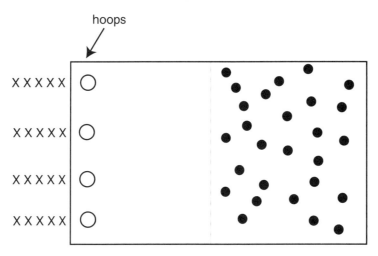

Milk Carton Soccer: Any indoor game or drill can make use of milk cartons instead of balls. All students can use the cartons, including special needs students—as seems best for your group.

Four-Square Soccer: Mark out an area with four adjoining 15´ × 15´ squares. Divide the class into four groups, and assign each to one square. One player from each team enters a square. Play begins as one player is given the ball and attempts to kick it out of an adjoining square. No ball may be kicked above knee height.

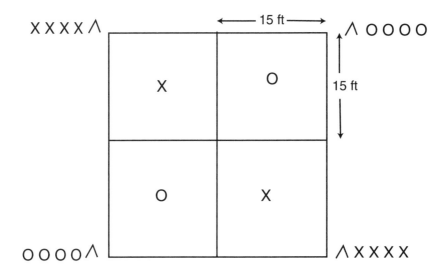

Use deflated soccer balls or milk cartons for special needs students. This is also an excellent opportunity to use a buddy to assist the special needs student. The buddy stands beside the student and attempts to trap balls kicked into their square, then passes the ball to the buddy who attempts the kick.

General Modifications:

Have the special needs student play a regular, or modified, game in a large circle in front of the goal. No other player can enter the circle to keep or steal the ball. Once in, the ball is passed or shot by the student. When indoors, all students can use gym scooters and play with a cage ball if a student is in a wheel chair.

Softball

Information for You

STUDY GUIDE FOR SOFTBALL

HISTORY

George W. Hancock of the Farragut Boat Club in Chicago developed softball in 1887. Hancock designed the game for indoor play with a sixteen-inch ball.

In 1895, Lewis Rober of the Minneapolis Fire Department adopted the game for outdoors using a twelve-inch ball with a cover similar to that of a baseball.

Softball has been called playground ball, kitten ball, recreation baseball, ladies baseball, and soft baseball.

In 1923, the National Recreation Association appointed a committee to study the variety of rules used and standardize them. In 1933, the Amateur Softball Association was founded. It is the governing body of the sport in the United States. The International Softball Federation was founded in 1952.

There are two classes of competition in softball—fast-pitch and slow-pitch. Fast-pitch softball has a nine-person team, and slow-pitch has a ten-person team. The tenth person in slow-pitch is a short fielder.

BENEFITS

1. Softball is an excellent co-ed activity.
2. Softball can be played by almost any age group and mixed ages.
3. Softball can be played on an outdoor area small enough to be accommodated on most playgrounds. Ground surface can be sand, dirt, or grass.
4. The only equipment needed is a softball, bat, glove (optional), and bases.
5. People can play softball with varying skill levels.

THE GAME

1. A team consists of ten players in slow-pitch, nine in fast-pitch.
2. A regulation game consists of 7 innings, or $6\frac{1}{2}$ if the team second at bat has scored more runs than its opponent.
3. One run is scored each time a runner legally touches all bases, in the correct order, and home plate before the third out is made.

ACTIVITY: SOFTBALL SKILL DRILLS

Focus/ Knowledge Skill	Equipment Needed	Suggested Grade Levels
Softball skills, including throwing, catching, batting, and base running, are presented in fun and challenging tasks.	Softballs for every 2 players 8 bats Cone markers Batting tees	Grades 4–8 Modifications for grade levels: Use soft balls, such as fleece balls or whiffle balls, for younger students.

Success Notes Keep students motivated by having them set goals at each station and rewarding the achievement of these goals.

MAKING IT WORK

Throwing—Overhand

Basic Throwing: Stand facing a partner and practice proper technique; elbow back, step toward the target with the opposite foot, throw, and follow through. Aim for the partner's chest. Start by standing 10 feet apart; after eight successful throws move back 5 feet, continuing until 20–25 feet apart.

Throw and Follow: Divide students into groups of five—four on bases and one "batter." The batter throws the ball to first and follows; the first-base person throws to second and follows. This rotation continues until the ball reaches the catcher, who then becomes the next batter.

Hit the Cone: Set a line of cone markers approximately 30 feet from the throwing line. Students stand behind the throwing line and, using tennis balls, throw at the cones. Each student takes five throws, then becomes the "ball return" and retrieves the balls, rolling them back to the line.

Fielding

Ground Ball-Fly Ball: Standing 15–20 feet from a partner, throw grounders and fly balls to each other. Stress proper position for catching: keeping the ball directly in front, bending at the knees and waist to catch the grounder, and keeping hands together when catching a fly ball.

106

Fielders' Relay:	Divide students into groups of three, and assign two groups to an area, standing in lines approximately 15 feet apart. The first player on one team takes the ball and throws a grounder to the first player in the opposite line, then runs to the back of the opposite line. The fielding player then throws a fly ball to the opposite line and follows to the end of that line. The rotation continues until all players are back in their original spots.

Base Running

Base Race:	Divide the class into two equal groups—one group standing behind home plate and the other behind second base. On the "go" signal, the first runners from each team begin running the bases. When they return to their original base, they touch the hand of the next runner, who runs the bases. The team that has all the players run the bases first is declared the winner.
Base Shuttle:	Divide the class into groups of six—each with two bases or cone markers placed 45 feet apart. On the "go" signal, the first player begins to run to the opposite base. When that runner touches the opposite base, the next runner goes. After the last runner in line touches the base, the first runner goes again. When all runners return to their original positions, the relay stops.

Batting

Ball Swing:	Suspend a whiffle ball on a string hanging from a wooden dowel attached to a basketball or volleyball stand. Adjust the height of the ball to be in the strike zone of the batter. As the batter hits the ball, it will swing around. The batter should stop the ball, set, and hit again.

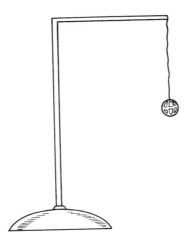

Hit and Run:	Using a "batting tee," the first student hits the ball and runs to first base. When the next batter hits and begins to run, the first batter runs back to home. Continue until all players have had a turn at bat.

ACTIVITY: AROUND THE BASES

Focus/ Knowledge Skill	Equipment Needed	Suggested Grade Levels
Softball skills of pitching, fielding, batting, and base running are put together in a variation of a regular softball game	1 softball, one bat, and a set of bases for each game played Protective equipment for the catcher	Grades 4–8 Modifications for grade levels: Younger students and those less skilled should use a batting tee.

Success Notes This game is fun, and it also enhances baseball skills and cooperation. To help eliminate confusion regarding runners being halfway to the next base, place a poly-spot between bases.

MAKING IT WORK

Divide students into groups of ten. One team begins as the batting team, the other as fielders. The fielders take infield and outfield positions, including catcher; the pitcher is a member of the batting team.

The game begins with the pitcher tossing the ball to the batter. When the ball is hit into the field, the batter runs to first base, circles the base (without touching it), and continues to the next base and circles it. As the runner is circling the bases, the fielder who catches the ball throws it to an infield player. All other defensive players run and line up behind that player, and players then pass the ball overhead until it reaches the end of the line. When the ball reaches the last player, she or he yells "Stop." This is the signal for the base runner to stop and proceed to the closest base. The next batter hits the ball and begins to run, as does any player on base.

There are no outs. After everyone has batted, the teams switch places.

Note: To keep everyone on the batting team involved, change pitchers after each batter.

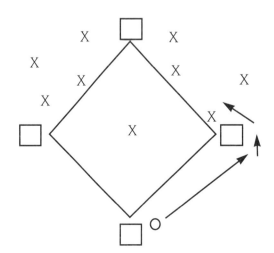

Fitness Activities	Skill Development	Games That Teach	Healthy Lifestyles	Keeping Track

ACTIVITY: RUN-FOR-FUN SOFTBALL

Focus/ Knowledge Skill	Equipment Needed	Suggested Grade Levels
Softball skills of batting, fielding, and throwing are emphasized in this fast-moving game.	1 softball, bat, bases, and catcher's mask for each field	Grades 4–8 Modifications for grade levels: For younger or less-skilled students, batting should be done from a tee.

Success Notes Keeping score in this game is almost impossible. Let the students know at the beginning that no score will be kept. Play for fun and skill development.

MAKING IT WORK

Divide the class into teams of eight each, and assign a batting and fielding team to each playing area. Teams can be larger, but it slows the activity and causes more waiting.

The first batter hits the ball and begins to run the bases as in regular softball. The fielding team retrieves the ball and plays it like a regular game—with the exception that there are no "force-outs."

Once a player reaches a base, that player does not have to run when a ball is hit. There is no limit to the number of players that may be on a base. (Make the base area large enough.) A runner who crosses home plate, gets an automatic free walk to first base.

After the last batter hits, all runners keep running until the catcher has control of the ball. Teams then switch positions.

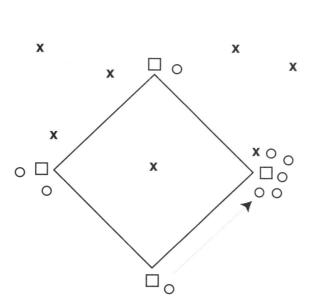

ACTIVITY: CROSS-COUNTRY SOFTBALL

Focus/ Knowledge Skill	Equipment Needed	Suggested Grade Levels
This activity is a combination of skill development and refinement in softball, and aerobic fitness development.	Softball, bat, catchers mask, bases for each playing area 8 cone markers per playing area	Grades 6–8 Modifications for grade levels: For individual students, placing the ball on a batting tee or cones may provide a greater opportunity for success.

Success Notes Depending on the ability level and aerobic endurance of groups, design the cross-country course so that all students can cover a minimum of three cones per attempt.

MAKING IT WORK

Design the playing area with a regular softball field and approximately eight cones arranged in a pattern around the playground. Divide the class into groups of seven to eight students, and assign two groups to each softball field. All teams can use the cross-country course cones.

This activity is played the same as a regulation softball game with two exceptions. First, there is a "one good pitch" rule. Second, any player who is "safe" on a base goes on a cross-country run.

After hitting and being safe, the player leaves the softball field and begins the cross-country run. The cross-country runner is attempting to pass as many cones as possible before the defense gets three outs. There may be several runners from a team running the course at the same time. After three outs are made, the runners add the total number of cones passed, which is their team's score for the inning.

Modification:

Place a hula hoop behind the pitcher's mound. If the ball is thrown to the pitcher and placed in the hoop before a runner is safely on a base, the runner is called out.

110

ACTIVITY: PITCHERS' DUEL

Focus/ Knowledge Skill	Equipment Needed	Suggested Grade Levels
Throwing accuracy for softball or baseball	5 balls for each target (whiffle or tennis balls) Cone marker or poly-spot for each target "Pitchers' Duel" target for each area Score card and pencil at each area	Grades 4–8 Modifications for grade levels: Throwing distances should be modified depending on grade and ability levels (40 ft. +, 4th grade to 55 ft. +, 8th grade).

Success Notes Have several throwing areas set up around the gym—each with different throwing distances. Allow students to practice in order to determine the best distance for their ability. Have a score card and pencil at each area. After reviewing scores, establish playing partners based on ability.

MAKING IT WORK

This is a challenging yet fun activity for students of all ages. Tape a "Pitchers' Duel" target at each station. Divide classes into groups of two to three each; assign two groups to each target.

To begin play, the first player throws a ball at the target. The result of the throw indicates the position of base runners. Another team member makes the next throw for the team. This rotation continues until 5 runs are scored or 2 outs are made, at which time the other team begins play. The "Pitchers' Duel" chart contains target areas for singles, doubles, triples, home runs, and outs. A player on base may advance 1 base ahead of the next "runner" until the first runner scores; for example, runner on first, next person throws a double, runner on first advances to third.

Play continues until a team has scored 15 runs or has played 3 complete innings, at which time teams rotate and begin play again.

PITCHER'S DUEL: TARGET DESIGN

Measurements: *48″ × 24″*

<table>
<tr><td rowspan="9">O
U
T</td><td align="center">Out</td><td rowspan="9">O
U
T</td></tr>
<tr><td align="center">Single</td></tr>
<tr><td align="center">Double</td></tr>
<tr><td align="center">Triple</td></tr>
<tr><td align="center">Home Run</td></tr>
<tr><td align="center">Double</td></tr>
<tr><td align="center">Single</td></tr>
<tr><td align="center">Out</td></tr>
</table>

SCORE CARD:

Team #_____

Inning	Runs Scored	Hits
1		
2		
3		

ACTIVITY: FAST BALL

Focus/ Knowledge Skill	Equipment Needed	Suggested Grade Levels
Skills including throwing and catching are used in a cooperative activity.	2 balls and 2 poly-spot or cone markers for each group of 15 students	Grades 4–7 Modifications for grade levels: For beginning students, use a fleece ball or whiffle ball.

Success Notes Stress cooperation and accuracy of throwing during this activity. All students must realize that if a ball is thrown in an area where it is not catchable, or is thrown too hard, it is their fault, not that of the receiver, if the ball is not caught.

MAKING IT WORK

Divide the class into groups of seven to eight with two groups assigned to each 40-foot playing area. Students form a circle, with opposing teams alternating positions. One person from each team comes to the center and stands by a marker facing opposite sides of the circle.

On the "go" signal, the center players throw the ball to their players on opposite sides of the circle; the catchers return the balls to the center players, who pass clockwise to the next teammates. The object is for one team to throw and catch the ball so fast that it overtakes the others team's ball. After each round, a new center player is selected from each team.

Variation:

To practice different throws, center players can be directed to throw underhand, overhand, grounders, flies, and so forth.

ACTIVITY: FIELDERS' CHOICE

Focus/ Knowledge Skill	Equipment Needed	Suggested Grade Levels
Fielding ground balls, throwing, and agility are emphasized in this relay activity.	Tennis ball or softball for each group Fitness cards for each group	Grades 4–8 Modifications for grade levels: Younger players, or those less skilled, should throw from a line 20 feet from the wall.

Success Notes Use a ball that is appropriate for the age and developmental level of the students. This is an excellent drill but should not be used for a lesson focus. Have groups participate in the activity for 4–5 minutes.

MAKING IT WORK

Divide students into groups of five to six—each assigned to a playing area. At each playing area, a poly-spot or cone should be placed 20–40 feet from the wall. This spot becomes the throwing line. Groups form a single file line behind the throwing line. The first player in line throws the ball against the wall. The next player fields the ball after one bounce, runs to the throwing line, and throws. This rotation continues for the duration of the activity. If a fielding player does not catch the ball after one bounce, that player runs to the "fitness card" area, draws a card, and returns to the group, where all players perform the activity listed. After the activity is completed, return the card to the Fitness Card area.

SAMPLE FITNESS CARDS

- All do 15 crunches.
- Pass the ball up and down the line 2 times.
- Give each member of the group a "high 5."
- All toss and catch the ball off the wall 10 times (5 feet away).

- All do 15 curl-ups.

- All do 15 push-ups.
- All run 1 lap.
- Jump rope for 1 minute.
- All do 25 skier jumps.
- All do 25 mountain climbers.
- Run to each group and say hello.

ACTIVITY: SOFTBALL CHALLENGE CIRCUIT

Focus/ Knowledge Skill	Equipment Needed	Suggested Grade Levels
Softball skills of throwing, catching, batting, and base running are reviewed in a fun and challenging activity.	1 softball for every 2 players 4 "foxtails," 4–6 tennis balls, 4 bats, 20 whiffle balls Cone markers or poly-spots	Grades 4–8 Modifications for grade levels: Narrow distances and lower targets for younger students.

Success Notes Motivate students by assigning a point value to each activity; for example, for each catch, a player gets 1 point. Players record their points at each station, trying to reach 1,000 points for the total circuit.

MAKING IT WORK

Arrange six challenge stations around the playing area, and then have students forms groups of four to six. Assign each group to a challenge station. On the "go" signal, groups work at their station for 5 minutes, then rotate to the next station.

Grounders: With partners facing each other 15 feet apart and one ball, throw grounders back and forth. After throwing in the center, throw to either side. After 10 throws, have one player throw the grounder, and the other field the ball and throw an accurate overhand return. Switch after 5 throws.

Quick Hands: One partner stands on a bench and holds one tennis ball in each hand. The other partner stands on the ground with hands behind the back. The first player holds the tennis balls in front and drops them. The second player tries to catch one in each hand before they hit the ground.

Accuracy Pitch: Using a hula hoop with a rope attached, place the rope over a basketball basket so it hangs approximately waist high. Students stand 20–30 feet away and attempt to throw—over- or underhand—at the hoop. After 10 throws, rotate players. (Have several retrievers for each hoop.)

115

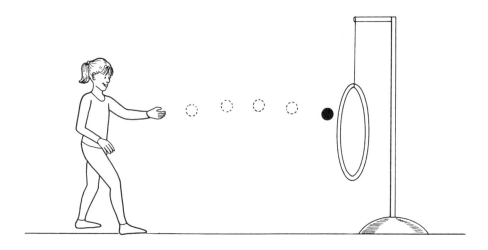

Over-the-Shoulder: Using a tennis ball, stand facing a wall 5 feet away. Throw the ball into the wall, hitting it approximately 10 feet above the ground. Immediately turn and try to catch the rebound over your shoulder. After they successfully complete this challenge, have partners stand side-by-side, one with a ball. The player with the ball says "Go," and the other one begins to run forward. The partner with the ball throws an arching toss over the shoulder of the runner, who attempts to make the catch.

"Foxtail" Catch: In groups of two, each with a "foxtail," one partner tosses a lob to the other partner standing 15 feet away. As the toss is made, a color (on the tail) is called. The receiving player attempts to catch the tail by the color called, then tosses a lob back, calling out a color.

Bat Speed: In groups of two, students stand at a batting tee with 5 balls and a bat (plastic). The first player to bat hits 5 balls into the wall, followed by the second player. After two rotations, players "choke up" on the bat to try to get more bat speed. Ask students if they can tell the difference—why would the bat go faster if it were shorter?

Additional Challenges to Consider

Pickle
Base Race
Hot Potato

ACTIVITY: CIRCLE SOFTBALL

Focus/ Knowledge Skill	Equipment Needed	Suggested Grade Levels
Batting, fielding, pitching, and catching are used in a fast-moving and challenging activity.	1 softball, bat, and catcher's mask for each playing area	Grades 4–6 Modifications for grade levels: For indoor play or less-skilled students, use a fleece ball or whiffle ball with a plastic bat.

Success Notes For safety and success, students should be reminded to stay outside the circle line prior to the ball's being hit.

MAKING IT WORK

Divide class into groups of eight to ten; assign two groups to each playing area. At each area, one cone marker, poly-spot, or base for each player on a team should be set in a circle formation (approximately 50 feet in diameter).

The object is for the batting team to hit the ball out of the circle formed by the fielding team. The members of each team are numbered. The pitcher is a member of the fielding team, with a number corresponding to the batter's; pitchers rotate with batters.

The batter stands approximately 5 feet in from the circle, with the pitcher moving in approximately 30 feet from the batter. Each batter attempts to hit 3 pitches out of the circle. After everyone has batted, sides exchange positions. One point is scored for each batted ball that gets outside the circle.

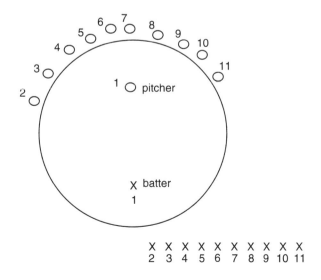

| Fitness Activities | Skill Development | Games That Teach | Healthy Lifestyles | Keeping Track |

ACTIVITY: INDOOR WHIFFLE BALL

Focus/ Knowledge Skill	Equipment Needed	Suggested Grade Levels
Softball skills of batting, fielding, and throwing are enhanced during this challenging activity.	1 whiffle ball 1 plastic bat Indoor/non-slip bases Catchers mask	Grades 4–8 Modifications for grade levels: Younger or less-skilled students may bat off a batting tee.

Success Notes Add motivation for those waiting to bat by having them jump rope, juggle, or dribble a basketball through cones. Give the batting extra points for the number of jump-rope turns, items juggled, or cones passed.

MAKING IT WORK

Divide the class into two equal teams—one batting, the other fielding. The fielding team takes up positions as in softball (extra players can go between first and second bases and in the outfield. No defensive players except the pitcher and catcher may be in front of the baseline. Although there is a pitcher on the fielding team, that pitcher is only a defensive player; the batting team supplies its own pitcher.

Each batter is given one "good" pitch and must take a full swing. If the batter misses, he or she is considered out. All hits are considered fair if they travel in front of home plate—off the walls, ceiling, or other objects can be played as a fair ball.

A caught fly ball does not count as an out. To get a runner out, the ball must be passed to first, second, and third base before the runner stops running. Any runner not on a base when the third base player controls the ball is out. A runner may stop at any base and there may be as many as three runners on a base at one time. Each team is allowed 2 outs per inning and no more than 10 runs.

ACTIVITY: SOFTBALL CRICKET

Focus/ Knowledge Skill	Equipment Needed	Suggested Grade Levels
Skills of batting, throwing, catching, and fielding are utilized in this activity. Students also become aware of the British game of cricket.	1 softball, 2 bats, 2 cone markers, and 2 bases at each field	Grades 6–8

Success Notes This is a great activity for all students. To enhance the experience, provide information related to the game of cricket. Ask students to describe the differences among softball, this activity, and cricket.

MAKING IT WORK

Divide students into groups of nine; assign two groups to each field. Each field is set with two bases approximately 25 feet apart, with a cone marker placed 3 feet behind each base.

The object of the game is for the batter to score by hitting the ball and running to the opposite base before the fielding team can throw the ball into the cone marker behind the batters base.

Students position themselves in an area between the bases but outside the baseline. One player from the batting team takes a position next to a base, and at the opposite end a pitcher from the same team takes a position by the opposite base. To start, the pitcher throws the ball, underhand, at the batter's cone marker. The batter attempts to protect the marker by hitting the ball. If the ball is hit—in any direction—the batter runs to the opposite base. The fielders try to field the ball, throw it from where it was recovered, and hit the cone while the runner is running. If the fielders do not hit the cone, the runner is safe and a point is scored. If the cone is hit, an out is recorded for the fielding team.

The play is repeated with the following batter. However, a player who is on the opposite base when the ball is hit runs back to the original base. Fielders may make try to hit either cone if two runners are moving. If both runners are safe, two points are scored. After 3 outs, the teams switch places.

Note: Rotate pitchers after five pitches. For variety, have the batters/runners rotate to the fielding positions after they have scored 2 runs (one at each base), or have been put out.

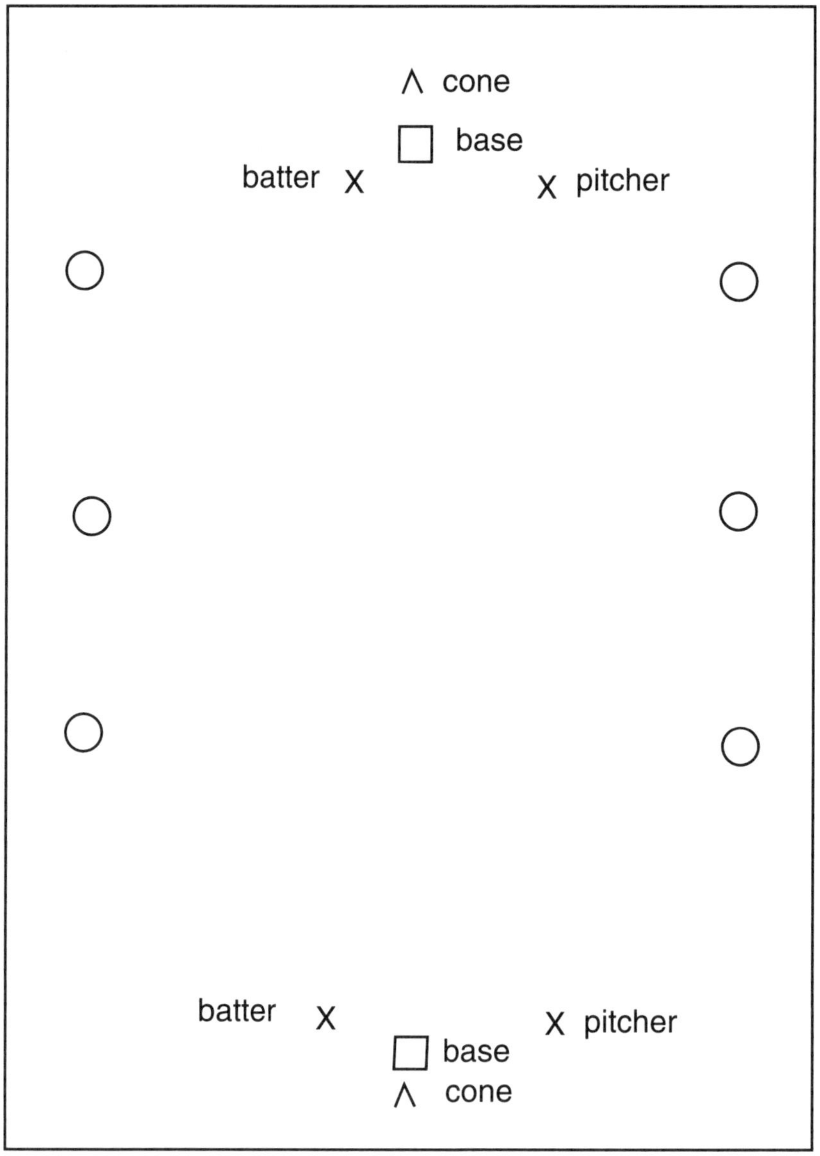
cone
base
batter
pitcher
batter
pitcher
base
cone

ACTIVITY: SOFTBALL ACTIVITIES FOR SPECIAL NEEDS STUDENTS

Focus/ Knowledge Skill	Equipment Needed	Suggested Grade Levels
Eye-hand coordination agility, basic coordination, and movement skills are enhanced through softball skills of throwing, catching, hitting, and running.	Plastic bats, yarn balls, whiffle balls, batting tee, beanbags, whiffle ball on a string All equipment should vary in size and color.	Grades 4–8

Success Notes A variety of experiences should be provided, with enough repetition at each developmental level. Using student buddies working as partners, or having special needs students working as a part of a small group, provides reinforcement of learned skills and a "safety net" for students.

MAKING IT WORK

Note: Providing developmentally appropriate activities for students will depend on their individual needs. Care must be taken to determine the appropriate activities and instructional formats that best meet individual abilities and needs. The following activities have been effective.

Instructional Progression

Throwing and catching skills should be practiced with a buddy using a variety of balls—yarn balls, brightly colored tennis balls, fleece balls, "Incrediballs®," and whiffle balls. Partners should begin from a close distance, moving back to a distance that is challenging but allows success.

Batting is an exciting activity for all students, including those with special needs. Using a whiffle ball suspended on a string attached to a stick, have students progress through the following activities:

1. Tap the stationary ball with the right and left hand. After successfully tapping, have students move their arms, using a batting motion and striking the ball with their hands.

2. Repeat the above progression with the ball swinging toward the student.

3. Using a plastic bat, have the student hit the ball as it swings across the body. Try batting on both the left and right side.

   Note: This is a great activity for a student in a wheelchair.

4. Repeat the above activity, placing the ball on a batting tee.

121

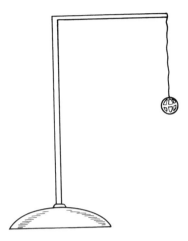

5. When practicing base running, arrange a series of poly-spots or cone markers in a line approximately 5–10 feet apart. Special needs students can run, wheel, crawl, or be assisted between markers.

6. Use a rebound net or pitch-back with beanbags, softballs, or—for throwing practice—5 1/2-inch playground balls. Vary the distance to throw, depending on the abilities of individual students.

Games and Drills

In the field, have special needs students play inside a circle, with a buddy, between first and second base or at mid-outfield. If the ball lands inside this area, the batter is automatically out.

When batting, using batting tees can make necessary accommodations.

When running the bases, try the following.

1. All defensive players must touch the ball before the runner makes it to first.

2. Make a short baseline inside the regular baseline.

3. If a special needs student makes it to first, he or she may stay there; other teammates pass the student, giving a "high five."

Recreational Sports

INFORMATION FOR YOU—STUDY GUIDES FOR

Tennis
Bowling
Golf
Badminton
Pickleball

- Racket Sport Relay
- Mat Pickleball
- Hand Pickleball
- Tennis Skill Challenge
- Relay Tennis
- Team Tennis
- Team Handball
- Bowling for Fun
- Skill Station Bowling
- Tic-Tac-Toe Archery
- Archery Baseball
- Over-the-Top Golf
- Pepper Golf
- Golf Croquet
- Racket Sports for Special Needs Students
- Golf Activities for Special Needs Students

Information for You

STUDY GUIDE FOR TENNIS

HISTORY

From the days of the ancient Greeks to the present, tennis has enjoyed great popularity. Tennis actually started as handball in Greece. In the Middle Ages it changed to a game of batting the ball with the open hand across a cord or over a mound of dirt. The early court was shaped like an hourglass, and the game was played with leather balls stuffed with hair. The type of racket has also changed from hands, to a glove, to a paddle, to a racket shaped like a snowshoe, and finally to its present style.

THE GAME

The idea of the game is to hit the ball with a racket over the net into the opposite court so that the opponents cannot return it. A game between two individuals is called singles; between teams of two, doubles.

Play begins when one player, standing behind the baseline, hits or serves the ball over the net so that it lands in the opponent's opposite service court. Before the serve is returned, the ball must bounce one time in the opponent's service court; after the return of the serve the ball may be hit either after the first bounce or before it bounces. The ball is hit back and forth until a player makes an error, by hitting the ball out-of-bounds, failing to hit the ball before it bounces twice, or failing to return it over the net.

The game is played to 4 points, with only the server being able to score a point. Points in the game are referred to by the following terminology:

0 points........................Love

1 point 15

2 points 30

3 points 40

4 points ....Game

The score of 40–40 is called deuce. If the score goes to deuce, one player must win two points in a row to win the game. The first point after deuce is called advantage, but if the player does not win the second consecutive point, the score goes back to deuce.

BASIC RULES

1. The server serves one whole game, then alternates with her or his opponent for the rest of the match.

2. The server stands behind the baseline and starts a game from the right side, serving into the opponent's right service court. The serve is made to alternate service courts throughout the game.

3. The server has two chances to serve into the proper service court on each point. If both serves fault, he loses the point.

4. The serve must bounce before the receiver may return it. All other balls may be hit before the bounce or after only one bounce.

5. Players switch sides on odd games—after the first, third, and fifth game.

6. After the serve, play or rally continues when

   • a ball lands within the boundaries of the playing court.

   • the ball is returned—even if outside the net posts—either above or below the level of the top of the net, provided it lands in the proper court, and even though it touches the net.

   • a ball hits the net, but passes over it, and lands in the proper court.

7. After the serve, players lose a point if

   • they fail to return the ball into the opponent's court.

   • they fail to return the ball before it bounces a second time.

   • they play the ball before it has passed the net.

   • they touch the ball with the body.

   • they contact the ball more than once with the racket during a stroke.

   • they throw the racket at and hit the ball.

Information for You

STUDY GUIDE FOR BOWLING

HISTORY

According to Sir Flinders Petrie, the oldest known form of bowling dates back to 5200 B.C., where, in the grave of an Egyptian child, they found equipment for playing a game similar to the sport of bowling. The earliest recorded game of bowling in the United States was in 1623, when it was played by settlers from Holland.

During the early days of the game, it was played outside on "bowling greens"; by 1840, many indoor bowling lanes existed around the New York City area. At that time, the game was played with nine pins arranged in a diamond shape. During these early days, gamblers exploited many people, therefore, laws were passed in New York and Connecticut that prohibited the game of ninepins. In order to continue playing the game, players added another pin, and the pin arrangement was changed from a diamond shape to a triangular one.

In 1895, the American Bowling Congress was formed and set up universal laws for the game. More than any other group, this organization is responsible for the continued growth and expansion of the game.

THE GAME

The American Bowling Congress rules state that the game shall use ten pins set in a triangular shape and shall consist of ten frames. Each player shall bowl two balls in each of the first nine frames, except when a strike is made. A player who scores a strike or spare in the tenth frame can deliver three balls.

It is easy to score a bowling game. A perfect score is 300 points. If all the pins are knocked down with the first ball, it is a strike. If all pins are knocked down with two balls, it is a spare. For a strike, the bowler is awarded 10 pins plus the total pinfall of the next two balls. For a spare, the award is 10 pins plus the pinfall of the next ball rolled. If a strike is made in the tenth frame, the next two balls are rolled immediately. If a strike or spare is not rolled, the score is the pinfall of the frame.

BASIC RULES

Players take their turn to bowl. Players bowl twice in each frame, unless all ten pins are knocked down with the first ball—a strike.

The ball must be rolled, with an underhand motion, down the lane. On delivery, the player must not touch or cross the foul line, even after releasing the ball. If the foul line is crossed, any pins knocked down are not scored. If the foul occurs in the first half of the frame, pins are reset and the second ball rolled. If the foul occurs in the second half of the frame, only those pins knocked down with the first ball are scored. A strike may not be scored with the second ball if a foul occurs in the first half of the frame.

Information for You

STUDY GUIDE FOR GOLF

HISTORY

Golf probably originated in Scotland, although its exact beginnings are not known. It is thought that shepherds tending to their sheep may have started the game by hitting stones with their staffs.

Golf was a popular game in Scotland in the fifteenth century. It was so popular that Parliament banned the sport in 1457, because the men were neglecting their practice of archery. The ban was soon forgotten when the King of Scotland, James IV, was found playing the game. Mary, Queen of Scots, was the first woman golfer in the history of the game. Golf continued to be popular among all people. The game was officially recognized in 1860, when the first British Open Tournament was played.

THE GAME

Golf is played with a small, hard ball, which is placed on the ground and hit with long-shafted clubs. The object of the game is to hit the ball from the teeing area to the green and into the 4″ cup with the fewest possible strokes.

Playing golf requires that the ball be hit long and short distances. These distances will vary from over 300 yards to a few inches. The ball must be hit from different areas, from short grass fairways, long grass areas (rough), sand, and the smooth putting green. Therefore, there are different types of clubs for the distance to be hit and the type of surface to be played from. In general, a wood will be used to hit long distances and irons lesser distances with greater loft. Irons are numbered 2 through 9 plus various wedges. The greater the number, the shorter the predicted distance and the higher the loft.

BASIC RULES

The basic rule of golf is that once you hit the ball from the tee, you may not touch it with your hand until you reach the green. The following are very basic rules; as you continue to play, you will learn more rules that govern specific situations.

1. To start each hole, the ball is teed from between set markers, or within two club lengths behind them.

2. After the first hole, the score on the previous hole determines play for the tee area. The player with the lowest score goes first, with the remaining players hitting in order of score, lowest to highest.

3. After players tee off, the ball farthest from the cup is played first.

4. The ball must be played "as it lies" on the grass or in the sand. Specific rules apply to some situations that allow the ball to be moved without penalty.

5. If the ball lies near an obstruction—sprinklers, hoses, benches, and so on—it may be moved but no closer to the cup.

6. Loose impediments, such as leaves or twigs, may be moved unless they are in a hazard.

7. In playing from a hazard, such as sand, the club may not touch the surface before the player swings and hits the ball.

8. The penalty for a lost ball or an unplayable ball is either (a) hit another ball from the spot where you played the first one and add a penalty stroke, or (b) drop a ball at any distance behind the point where the ball lies, and add a penalty stroke.

9. If a ball goes out-of-bounds, another shot must be taken from the place where the first ball was played.

SAFETY

1. Before taking any swings, check the area to see that no one is near enough to be accidentally hit.

2. When playing, never walk ahead of anyone making a shot.

3. If a ball you have hit may possibly strike someone, yell "Fore" loudly.

Information for You

STUDY GUIDE FOR BADMINTON

HISTORY

Badminton was first known as "Poona" which was the name of a town in India where British Army officers first saw and played the game. In the late 1800s, the officers brought the game to England. The game became quite popular in England and was renamed when the Duke of Beaufort brought the game to his estate called "Badminton House." The popularity of the game spread throughout the world. It became a popular American game in the early 1930s, with the American Badminton Association founded in 1937.

BENEFITS

Badminton is a great leisure activity that requires little equipment and can be played in or out of doors, by people of all ages and skill levels.

GENERAL RULES

1. All serves for a side begin on the right side of the court. If a point is made, the following serve is from the left side. Serves continue to alternate sides as long as one player or team has the serve.

2. Only the serving team may score points. If they make a fault, they lose the serve; this is known as a "hand down." A team is allowed two "hand downs" before the serve goes to their opponents.

3. The short service line and the line dividing the two service courts are in effect only during the service.

4. All serves are made diagonally. The shuttle must clear the short service line and be within the receiver's service court to be considered good. This rule applies to both singles and doubles.

5. A fault is made if

   a. the server contacts the shuttle higher than the server's waist.

   b. in serving, the shuttle falls into the wrong service court, or lands before the short service line or beyond the long service line.

   c. the server lifts his or her feet while serving, or stands outside the service court when serving.

   d. the shuttle fails to pass over the net, or a player touches the net.

   e. a player hits the shuttle twice.

6. Games are to 15 points.

STRATEGY

- Anticipate all returns. Hit the shuttle back to the court area your opponent is leaving.

- Plan your strokes ahead and change the pace of the game often.

- Always play the shuttle in front of you.

- When playing doubles (side-by-side) each player is responsible for half of the court (up and back)—one player at the net and the other covering the back court—or (combination) side-by-side. Side-by-side play is used for defense, and up and back for offense.

Information for You

STUDY GUIDE FOR PICKLEBALL

HISTORY
Pickleball was created during the summer of 1965 on Bainbridge Island, Washington. The game was developed by U.S. Congressman Joel Pritchard, along with William Bell and Barney McCallum. The original purpose of the game was to provide a sport for the entire family that could be played in backyards or in driveways. Since the mid 1970s, pickleball has grown from a backyard family game to a formalized court game played around the world.

COURT SIZE
The official pickleball court measures 20 feet × 44 feet for both singles and doubles. The net is 56 inches on the ends, but hangs down to 34 inches in the center.

RULES
The rules of pickleball are similar to those for badminton. When serving, the player must keep one foot behind the back line. The serve is made with an underhand stroke, with the paddle passing below the waist. The server must drop the ball and hit it before it bounces. The hit ball must cross to the opposite side of the court, and it must clear the "nonvolley" zone. Only one serve attempt is allowed, unless the ball hits the net on the serve and lands in the proper service court, in which case the serve is repeated.

At the start of each new game, the first serving team is allowed only one fault before giving up the ball to their opponents. Thereafter, both members on each team will serve and fault before the ball is turned over to the opposing team. When the receiving team wins the serve, the player in the right-hand court will always serve first.

Each team must play the first shot off a bounce; the receiving team must let the serve bounce, and the serving team must let the return bounce before playing it. After the "bounce" shots have occurred, the ball may be either played off the bounce or volleyed.

A "volley" means that the ball is hit in the air before it bounces. All volleying must be done with players' feet behind the nonvolley zone line. It is a fault if a player steps into the zone and volleys, or steps over the line on the follow-though.

A fault occurs when a player hits the ball out-of-bounds, steps into the nonvolley zone when volleying the ball, or volleys the ball before it has bounced once on each side of the net, or if the ball does not clear the net.

SCORING

Only the serving team may score a point. A player who is serving continues to serve until that team makes a fault. The game is played to 11 points, with the winning team doing so by 2 points.

Remember that pickleball is a sport where shot placement, control, and tactics are of greater importance than power or strength.

COURT DESIGN

	Baseline
Sideline	Sideline
NONVOLLEY ZONE	
NONVOLLEY ZONE	NET
Sideline	Sideline
	Baseline

ACTIVITY: RACKET SPORT RELAY

Focus/ Knowledge Skill	Equipment Needed	Suggested Grade Levels
Focus can vary depending on the sport being played—badminton, pickleball, or tennis. The object is to demonstrate agility and the skills necessary to volley.	1 racket or paddle per player 1 appropriate court for each group of 8 (4 per team. 1 ball, or badminton birdie for each court	Grades 6–8 Modifications: Establish a time limit for play rather than playing to an ending score.

Success Notes When assigning groups, special attention should be given to assigning competitors of similar abilities. Place emphasis on moving and cooperating with others in the group.

MAKING IT WORK

Divide the class into groups of four and assign two groups to each court. One player from each group takes position on the court. Other members of the group form a line behind the end line.

The "server" stands in the appropriate court and performs a regulation serve, then immediately leaves the court and goes to the end of the team's line, being replaced by the next team member in line. The "receiver" returns serve and goes to the end of that line, being replaced by the next member of the team. This rotation continues until an error is made. If a player's hit scores a point, the next player in line comes onto the court to serve.

Score is kept as in the regulation game and is governed by regular rules.

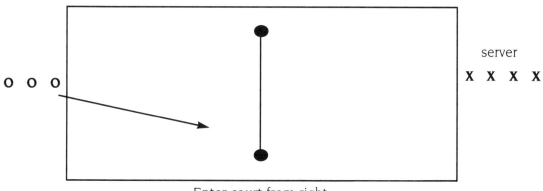

Enter court from right;
leave from left.

ACTIVITY: MAT PICKLEBALL

Focus/ Knowledge Skill	Equipment Needed	Suggested Grade Levels
Basic pickleball skills of serving and volleying	4´ × 8´ or 5´ × 10´ folding mats— one mat for every two students (mark a playing area approximately 1 foot on both ends and 10 feet deep on each side) Pickleball paddles for each student and 1 pickleball for every pair	Grades 4–6

Success Notes If enough mats are not available to have all students playing, "short courts" can be made by placing "Caution" tape between two cones. Don't worry about net height; the purpose is to have students able to volley and control the ball.

MAKING IT WORK

Have students get in pairs—each assigned to a folded mat or short court. Review the basic skills of pickleball, stressing ball control. Control is gained by having the face of the paddle facing the direction the ball is to go. Also stress that the object of this activity is not to "beat" or make your partner miss, but to have an extended rally.

To begin the serving, students must drop the ball and serve. Prior to making a return, the receiving player must let the ball bounce. After the initial exchange, the ball may be played before bouncing. In this activity there is no nonvolley zone.

After 3 minutes of play, players rotate to different partners. Prior to the actual rotation, team points may be awarded for the longest volley, or to any pair having an extended volley of more than 20 hits.

When new partners are at their mat or short court, play resumes with another rotation after 3 minutes.

Note: This is an excellent activity to be used in combination with "Mat Circuit" fitness development activities.

134

ACTIVITY: HAND PICKLEBALL

Focus/ Knowledge Skill	Equipment Needed	Suggested Grade Levels
Basic striking skills, which lead up to using a paddle or racket	Short courts measuring approximately 10′ × 15′ on both sides of the net Pickleball net and support stands or cones with a piece of "Caution" tape placed between them One softball-size plastic whiffle ball or $8\frac{1}{2}$-inch rubber playground ball for each court	Grades 4–6 Modifications for grade levels: Use an $8\frac{1}{2}$-inch rubber playground ball for lower grades and less-skilled players

Success Notes Don't worry about net height; the purpose is to have students able to gain proper hitting position and to volley, control the ball, and cooperate with a partner.

MAKING IT WORK

Group students into pairs, and assign two pairs to a court. Groups should position themselves to play a doubles match.

Play begins as in a regulation pickleball game. The server must serve from the right service court by bouncing the ball and striking it, using an open hand, with an underhand motion. Once the serve has bounced in the opposite court, it may be returned by striking it with an open hand. (**Note:** A variation that provides for greater success allows the ball to be hit twice by the returning team before it crosses the net.) Play continues until the ball is not returned, goes out-of-bounds, or fails to clear the net on the serve. Only the serving team scores points.

Play continues until one team has reached 11 points, winning by 2, or play has continued for 10 minutes. After each game, teams rotate to other courts.

ACTIVITY: TENNIS SKILL CHALLENGE

Focus/ Knowledge Skill	Equipment Needed	Suggested Grade Levels
Various tennis skills—forehand, backhand, volley, and agility—are included in this individual challenge activity. Goal setting can also become a part of this activity.	Tennis racket and ball for each group of 2 Wall target, cone markers, score sheets, pencils	Grades 5–8 Modifications for grade levels: Vary the distance on the wall volley, depending on skill level of students.

Success Notes This activity can also be done in the gym using indoor foam tennis balls. Use this activity as a culminating challenge before beginning to play matches. When completing the score cards, partners combine their individual scores.

MAKING IT WORK

Arrange ten stations around the playing area as follows:

1. **Target Serve** Students stand 20 feet from the target (suspended hula hoop or wall target). Using a drop serve or overhand serve, record the number of times the target is hit in 1 minute.

2. **Forehands** Standing 20 feet from the wall, how many forehands can be hit in 1 minute?

3. **Backhands** Standing 20 feet from the wall, how many backhands can be hit in 1 minute?

4. **Forehand Volley** Standing 20 feet from the wall, how many consecutive forehand volleys can be hit in 1 minute?

5. **Backhand Volley** Standing 20 feet from the wall, how many consecutive backhand volleys can be hit in 1 minute?

6. **Ups** Starting with the ball balanced on the racket, how many times can the ball be hit up in 1 minute?

7. **Downs** Bounce the ball and maintain the bounce. How many down hits can be made in 1 minute?

8. **Agility Run** Starting on one line, run, with the racket, to a line 30 feet away, touch it with the racket, and run back to the start line. How many lines can be touched in 1 minute?

9. **Partner Toss—Forehand** With a partner standing 15 feet away, how many tosses, hits, and catches can be made in 1 minute?

136 10. **Partner Toss—Backhand** With a partner standing 15 feet away, how many tosses, hits, and catches can be made in 1 minute?

TENNIS CHALLENGE SCORE CARD

Name: _____

STATION	SCORE		BONUS	TOTAL POINTS
Target Serve		plus	5 points	_____
Forehands		times	2	_____
Backhands		times	3	_____
Forehand Volley		plus	7 points	_____
Backhand Volley		plus	10 points	_____
Ups		divide by	2	_____
Downs		divide by	3	_____
Agility Run		times	5	_____
Partner Toss—Forehand		plus	6	_____
Partner Toss—Backhand		plus	8	_____

Total _____

ACTIVITY: RELAY TENNIS

Focus/ Knowledge Skill	Equipment Needed	Suggested Grade Levels
Basic tennis strokes combined with agility and cooperation in a fast-moving and challenging game.	Tennis racket for each student 1 tennis ball for each court Cone markers	Grades 6–8

Success Notes This activity can be done either on a court across a net or in the gym against a wall. Players must remember to move off the court quickly after hitting so they don't interfere with teammates.

MAKING IT WORK

Indoors or against a wall:

Each playing station should include a starting line approximately 20 feet from the wall and a line on the wall 3 feet from the ground. Place two cone markers 10 feet apart at each station. Arrange students in groups of four, with two groups at each playing station—each group standing behind a cone.

To begin, a player from one team starts with a drop-hit to the wall above the line. Then, alternating teams, each student in turn hits the ball before it bounces two times or goes past the cone markers. Points are scored as in regular tennis. After each set (6 games), teams switch sides.

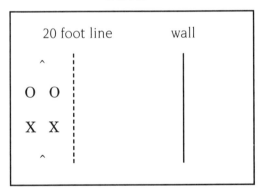

Indoor

Outdoors or across a net:

The playing area is half of a regulation tennis court; two playing groups are using each court. Rather than having opposing groups stand next to each other, in the outdoor/net variation, opposing groups stand on opposite sides of the net. Play and scoring are the same as in the indoor/wall game.

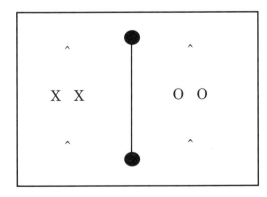

Outdoor

ACTIVITY: TEAM TENNIS

Focus/ Knowledge Skill	Equipment Needed	Suggested Grade Levels
Using various strokes in a fast-moving game involving teamwork and agility	Tennis racket for each student 1 ball for each court	Grades 6–8 Modifications: This activity may also be used for indoor tennis.

Success Notes Prior to participating in this fast-moving activity, students should develop the basic forehand and backhand skills.

MAKING IT WORK

Students are divided into groups and assigned to a court—half of the students on one side the other half on the other side. To begin, one student from each group enters the court.

Play begins as one student puts the ball into play using a "friendly" serve (ball is dropped and hit after the bounce) into the opponent's court. After hitting the ball, the player leaves the court and is replaced by the next player in line, who attempts a return. This rotation continues by both teams after each successful hit. If an error occurs, the player hitting the ball leaves the court and is replaced by the next person in line, who picks up the ball and puts it into play using a friendly serve. Points are scored as in regular tennis.

Note: Students waiting in line should be far enough to the rear of the court not to interfere with a hit.

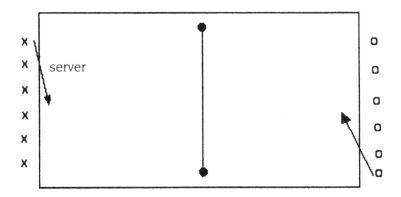

ACTIVITY: TEAM HANDBALL

Focus/ Knowledge Skill	Equipment Needed	Suggested Grade Levels
Accurate throwing, catching, agility, general defensive skills, and cooperation are enhanced.	1 Gatorskin® or rhythmic gymnastic-type ball (6˝) Colored pinnies for one team 2 folding mats (goals)	Grades 6–8

Success Notes Stress team play and passing. As some students will have to wait while others are participating, have an alternative challenge for them—juggling, jump-rope tricks, partner challenges, and so forth.

MAKING IT WORK

The object of the game is to throw the ball into the opponents' goal from outside the "shooting line." The game is played on a regular basketball court, with one goal placed under the basket at each end. A shot may be taken only by an offensive player standing outside the key. The goalie is the only player from either team who may be in the key forward of the foul line.

Divide students into teams of six players each. Two teams take random positions on the court with one player from each team entering the center circle for a jump ball. Play begins with a jump ball. Once control is gained, a team must complete three passes before a shot may be taken. Any time control of the ball changes hands, three passes must be completed prior to a shot being taken. A player who has control of the ball may hold it for only three seconds and may take only three running steps before passing. Passes may be direct or indirect using a wall to pass off.

If there is a foul (basketball rules) or rule violation (traveling, not enough passes, entering the goal box) a free direct pass is awarded. After a goal is scored, the ball is brought back to the center circle for a jump ball.

Hint: Rotate teams every 3 minutes regardless of the number of goals scored.

Fitness Activities	Skill Development	Games That Teach	Healthy Lifestyles	Keeping Track

ACTIVITY: BOWLING FOR FUN

Focus/ Knowledge Skill	Equipment Needed	Suggested Grade Levels
Basic bowling skills are introduced and refined in a recreational activity.	1 indoor bowling set (10 pins and indoor ball) for every 4–5 students Folding mats Pencils and score sheet for each lane	Grades 4–8 Modifications for grade levels: Shorten the distance between pins and foul line for younger students.

Success Notes Begin this activity without keeping score. Modify the rules to allow students to roll two balls per frame, even if a strike is made. As the class gains experience, keep a team score; each team members' scores are added together after each frame.

MAKING IT WORK

Divide the class into teams of four or five students. Assign each to a lane and a starting position; bowler, pin setter, ball return (if five per group add a second pin setter). After players are in position, the game is ready to begin.

On the "go" signal the groups begin, using the following format:

- All bowlers get two balls per frame.
- After the first roll, the pin setter removes pins knocked down
- The ball returner picks up the ball, sprints back to the bowler, and hands it to him or her for the next delivery. The bowler may not begin until the returner is back standing on a mat.
- After the second ball is rolled, the pins are set, the ball returner sprints back and becomes the bowler, the bowler becomes the pin setter, and the pin setter becomes the ball returner.
- If five players are at each lane, two pin setters are used, and they rotate from second setter to first setter.

Variation:

Bring a fitness component to the game by having the bowler sprint to a spot behind the bowling line after the roll while the ball returner is returning the ball.

141

ACTIVITY: SKILL STATION BOWLING

Focus/ Knowledge Skill	Equipment Needed	Suggested Grade Levels
This activity incorporates the enhancement of bowling skills in combination with skill- and fitness-development stations.	1 gym bowling set (10 pins and 1 ball) for every 4–5 students Folding mat at each lane Equipment required for skill/fitness-development activities.	Grades 4–8 Modifications for grade levels: Vary the skill/fitness stations, based on the skill level and emphasis for each class.

Success Notes This activity provides an excellent opportunity to review skill previously taught while students are participating in a recreational activity. When arranging skill/fitness stations, make sure there are activities at which all can succeed.

MAKING IT WORK

Divide the class into groups of five or six and assign each to a bowling lane. The bowling format described in "Bowling for Fun" should also be used with this activity.

Skill/fitness development stations are set on the opposite side of the gym from each bowling lane. Following the "Bowling for Fun" format, the rotation is modified to include station work.

- To begin, assign one (two if six per group) player from each lane to the skill/fitness station. While the remainder of the group is bowling, the students at the station work on the assigned tasks.
- After completing a frame, the bowler rotates to the station, and the station player moves to pin setter.

After all groups have completed a full rotation at their lane and station, all groups rotate to their left one lane or station, with the group at the left end moving to the right end.

Sample Skill/Fitness Stations

- Juggling: Scarves, flower sticks, or other items
- Bench steps
- Basketball—spot shot
- Rope-skipping routine
- Volleyball—wall volley
- Basketball—figure 8 dribble

142

ACTIVITY: TIC-TAC-TOE ARCHERY

Focus/ Knowledge Skill	Equipment Needed	Suggested Grade Levels
Archery skills used in a fun and motivational format	Bows and arrows for each group of 2 students 2 cone markers, tic-tac-toe target, pencil, and score card at each shooting area	Grades 6–8 Modifications for grade levels: Shorten the distance between shooting area and target for less-skilled students

Success Notes Safety is the major concern in this activity. To facilitate success and promote safety, have the shooter standing between shooting cones, and the spotter 5 feet behind. After all arrows are shot, the bow is laid down and students sit or kneel. When all groups have finished and are sitting, arrows are retrieved, students return to their area and wait for the "ready" signal.

MAKING IT WORK

Place a tic-tac-toe playing board on each target. Students stand in groups between cones at each station. On the "ready" signal, the first student in each group picks up the bow and one arrow. On the "shoot" signal, that person shoots the arrow, attempting to land in a tic-tac-toe square. On the next signal, the next player in each group attempts a shot. This rotation continues until each student has shot four arrows or has won a tic-tac-toe game.

As one partner is shooting, another acts as a spotter and records the hit on a paper tic-tac-toe matrix at the shooting area.

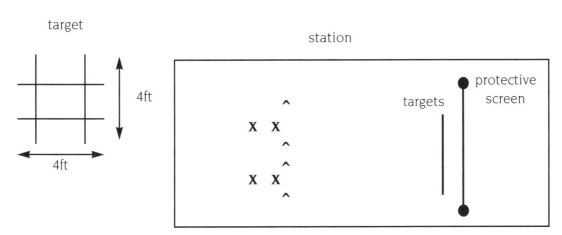

target

4ft

4ft

station

targets

protective screen

143

ACTIVITY: ARCHERY BASEBALL

Focus/ Knowledge Skill	Equipment Needed	Suggested Grade Levels
Archery skills are used in a motivational team activity.	1 bow and 10 arrows for each shooting area 2 cone markers baseball field target, and score card for each shooting area	Grades 6–8 Modifications for grade levels: Shorten the distance between shooting area and target for less-skilled students.

Success Notes Safety is the major concern in this activity. To facilitate success and promote safety, have the shooter stand between shooting area cones, and the spotter 5 feet behind. After all of the groups' arrows are shot, the bow is laid down and students sit or kneel. When all groups have finished and are sitting, arrows are retrieved, and students return to their area and wait for the "ready" signal.

MAKING IT WORK

Place a baseball playing board on each target, students in groups of four (two teams consisting of two players each) stand between cones at each station. On the "ready" signal, the first student in each pair picks up the bow and one arrow. On the "shoot" signal, the first player shoots the arrow, attempting to land in a hit area. On the next signal, the partner attempts a shot. This rotation continues until 3 outs are made or all 10 arrows have been shot. After the "inning" is completed, the total number of runs is counted.

After arrows have been retrieved, students return to the shooting area and wait for the "ready" signal. On signal, the opposing team begins shooting. This rotation continues for 9 innings or 20 minutes. After the game is completed, scores are added.

Other Motivational Ideas

Use balloons at various locations on the target. Put "reward" notes in several balloons; for example, free pop, 10 points, and 1 game ticket. Students hitting the balloon get the card and reward.

Try having a class piñata with candy or healthy snacks inside. Hang the piñata in front of a target, have all students shoot on signal, trying to hit and break the piñata. When it is broken students follow the established safety rules, wait, and get the rewards on signal.

Archery Baseball Target

3ft

out

single

double

home run

4ft   out   out

triple

single

out

ACTIVITY: OVER-THE-TOP GOLF

Focus/ Knowledge Skill	Equipment Needed	Suggested Grade Levels
Accuracy and controlled hitting are combined in an individual or team activity.	1 golf club—9 iron or wedge for each group of 2 players 4 tennis or baseball-size whiffle balls, or golf balls for each group	Grades 5–8 Modifications for grade levels: Use tennis or softball-size whiffle balls for less-skilled players.

Success Notes Stress control and accuracy of each shot. Place an end line approximately 30 yards from the starting line. No ball may pass over that line.

MAKING IT WORK

Arrange each group along a starting line behind a cone marker. To begin play, the first player hits one ball. The next player from each team then hits a ball that must land past the first ball. This rotation continues until each player has hit two balls.

Regardless of the distance, the first ball hit is the initial target. Any ball hit past the boundary line or that fails to pass the prior shot is out of play.

Award 1 point for each ball passed on a roll, and 3 points if the target ball is passed in the air. If all balls are passed in the air and remain within the boundaries, award a bonus of 5 points.

After each group has hit all balls, students lay the clubs on the ground, run out and retrieve the balls, return to their hitting position, and wait for the "start" signal.

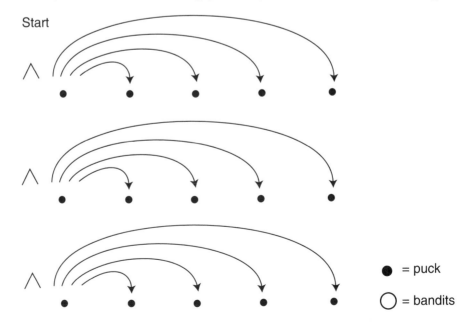

Start

● = puck

○ = bandits

Fitness Activities	Skill Development	Games That Teach	Healthy Lifestyles	Keeping Track

ACTIVITY: PEPPER GOLF

Focus/ Knowledge Skill	Equipment Needed	Suggested Grade Levels
Fundamental grip and swing techniques, combined with accuracy in chipping and cooperation	1 golf club—9 iron or wedge for each group of 2 2 tennis-/or baseball-size size whiffle balls per group 2 cone markers and 1 hula hoop per group	Grades 5–8

Success Notes Stress basic swing fundamentals for chip and short shots. Remind players that accuracy is rewarded in golf.

MAKING IT WORK

Assign each group of students to a hitting area. One partner stands between the cones while the other stands in a hoop approximately 20 feet away. On the "go" signal, players begin hitting to the partner, who catches it (catchers must keep one foot within the hoop), and tosses it back to the partner. If the catcher fails to catch the ball, the hitter hits another. Players stop after the catcher misses two balls or hitter has five hits. After all players have finished hitting, partners switch places.

As players become more accurate, move the targets back to 30 feet, or even 60 feet.

Note: Score can be kept by awarding 1 point for each ball caught in a legal manner (one foot in the hoop). Award bonus points for catching five consecutive balls.

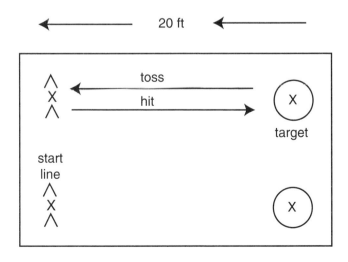

ACTIVITY: GOLF CROQUET

Focus/ Knowledge Skill	Equipment Needed	Suggested Grade Levels
Basic golf swing and hitting for accuracy—pitch shots. Focus on proper form and hitting under control for accuracy.	Golf club—9 iron or wedge for each group of 2 players 1 whiffle, tennis, or golf ball for each student 20 cone markers or flags and 10 hula hoops Golf Croquet" score card	Grades 5–8 Modifications for grade levels: Use whiffle or tennis balls for younger or less-skilled players.

Success Notes As with all golf activities, safety must be stressed: Stand outside and behind the hitting area when waiting your turn, never hit until the group in front has moved from the target area, carry the club by the head and never swing it while walking.

MAKING IT WORK

This game is played within a boundary area—objective being to hit the ball from one set of markers to the next, staying within the boundary. Prior to beginning play, arrange the course using cone markers and hoops.

Each group begins at a different location, with the first player attempting to hit the ball from the start area to the next target while staying within the boundary. If the

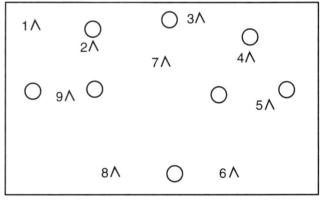

ball goes out of the marked area, it must be retrieved, with a one-stroke penalty, and played from the nearest point in bounds. If hit by another player's ball, it must be taken back to the start marker and played with no additional penalty stroke. Students count each stroke until they reach the target on the last hole. The object is to complete the course with the fewest number of strokes.

Score Card

player	1	2	3	4	5	6	7	8	9	total

ACTIVITY: RACKET SPORTS FOR SPECIAL NEEDS STUDENTS

Focus/ Knowledge Skill	Equipment Needed	Suggested Grade Levels
Striking an object with right, left, or both hands; extensions of the hand with various rackets; eye-hand coordination and perceptual development	All equipment should vary in size and color Various rackets: short-handle badminton and tennis rackets, whiffle rackets, and ping-pong paddles. Whiffle balls on strings, assorted size badminton birdies (separate and on strings), Nerf™ balls, balloons, and a 6′ × 1″ pole with clip	Grades 4–8

Success Notes A variety of experiences should be provided, with enough repetition at each developmental level. Using student buddies working as partners, or having special needs students working as a part of a small group, provides reinforcement of learned skills and a "safety net" for students.

MAKING IT WORK
Note: To ensure success of all students, individual needs must be considered. The activities listed have proven successful with various categories of special needs students.

Activity Progression
Begin with basic eye-hand coordination and perceptual activities. Hang a whiffle ball from a string and have students perform the following:

1. Begin with using both hands and progress to right and left. Tap the ball back and forth several times. Repeat this skill to gain motor control and tempo.

2. Repeat the progression listed above, using a paddle or short-handle racket. For some students, Velcro™ may be used to help hold the racket in position.

3. Move to using a balloon, and repeat activities 1 and 2 while tossing the balloon to the student.

4. With a short-handle racket or paddle, toss a large brightly colored Nerf™ ball. Work on tempo of the toss and strike.

5. Adapt a racquet game by making the court smaller or larger. Change the scoring format, lower the net, or move the service line forward to allow for greater success.

6. Use partners to support and assist special needs students, and let them think of other modifications to make the experience a success.

149

ACTIVITY: GOLF ACTIVITIES FOR SPECIAL NEEDS STUDENTS

Focus/ Knowledge Skill	Equipment Needed	Suggested Grade Levels
Eye-extended hand coordination skills, goals setting, and recreational safety through golf skill modifications	All items should vary in size, color, and shape. Adapt the golf club by making it shorter, longer, or bigger striking surface, or bending it to meet individual needs. Hockey sticks of varying size, plastic whiffle balls, tennis balls, Nerf™ soccer balls, plastic or paper cups, gym mats and/or rug squares.	Grades 4–8

Success Notes Working with another student or students (buddy system) and in small groups provides both support and assistance to special needs students. A variety of experiences should also be provided to stimulate students and maintain interest. Determine the potential for success with each student, and build upon this foundation.

MAKING IT WORK

Providing for each individual student's adaptation will require numerous modifications and is dependent upon individual student needs.

The first activity to introduce is putting. The focus should be on moving the ball various distances—long and short—and on accuracy. Use a large target, such as a hula hoop, to begin with. After the basic stroke has been taught, add obstacles to the hole or putting course. Use partners and reward best ball or team high point.

Moving to chipping and hitting, use a short (half) swing so greater success may be achieved. Chip the ball off a rug square or mat and over gym mats placed approximately 5 feet in front of the player.

Special needs students should actively participate in lead-up game situations with other students. Appropriate activities may be found in this section or by contacting your local PGA Regional Section Youth Director or a local golf professional.

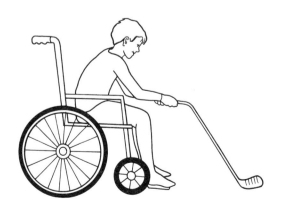

Volleyball

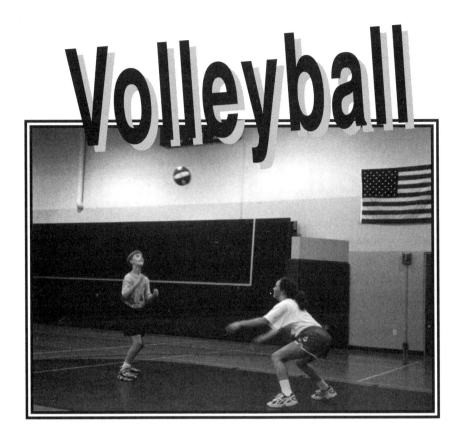

- Information for You—Study Guide for Volleyball

- Volleyball Skill Drills

- Four-Square Volleyball—Low Net

- Target-Set Relay

- Three-on-Three Line Volleyball

- Rotation Volleyball

- Hoop-Target Volleyball

- Alternative-Station Volleyball

- Crazy Ball

- Leader of the Court

- Team Pass

- Backboard Set

- Volleyball Activities for Special Needs Students

Information for You

STUDY GUIDE FOR VOLLEYBALL

HISTORY

Volleyball is one of the few popular games developed in the United States. In 1895, William Morgan, while working in a YMCA in Holyoke, Massachusetts, developed it as a team game to play indoors. Morgan first used a tennis net stretched about 6 1/2 feet from the floor. For a ball, he first tried the bladder of a basketball, but that was too light and slow. Finally he decided on a ball similar to the present volleyball, and a sporting goods company made one for him.

The object of the game was to keep the ball going back and forth over the net without its touching the floor. At first, the game was divided into innings, and any number of people could play on a team. In 1924, rules were published. In 1928, the United States Volleyball Association was formed, and this Association developed rules as they currently exist.

THE COURT AND GAME

Volleyball is played on a court 30 feet wide by 60 feet long. A net 7 feet, $4\frac{1}{4}$ inches from the floor divides the court. A team consists of six players: left, center, and right forwards; left, center, and right backs. The player in the right back position is the server. Only the serving team may score points. If the receiving team fails to legally return the ball over the net, a point is awarded. When the serving team fails to serve the ball into the opponents' court, or return the ball into the opponents' court, a "side-out" is called, and the other team becomes the serving team. A game is completed when one team has scored a total of 15 points and has a 2-point lead. The team that is first to win two out of three games is the winner of a match.

RULES

1. The server may not touch the end line while serving the ball. The ball may not touch the net on the serve.

2. When playing the ball, the player must clearly hit the ball—not "carry" it.

3. The ball must be played before it touches the ground.

4. The boundary lines are considered "in." Therefore, a ball that lands on or touches part of any line should be played.

5. Other than on the serve, it is legal for the ball to touch the net.

152

6. No player may touch the opponents' court.

7. No player may touch the net. Players may, however, reach over the net on the follow-through of a hit.

8. Players may leave their own court to play a ball, but may not enter the opponents' court.

9. Each team may hit the ball as many as three times before returning it to the opponents' court.

10. No player may hit the ball twice in succession. A player may play the ball on the first and third hit.

BASIC SKILLS

1. *Serving:*   Underhand, overhand.

2. *Volleying:* Overhead Set—This is most often used to pass the ball to a teammate.
Bump—Most commonly is used to receive serves, spiked balls, or net recoveries.

3. *Spiking:*   The spike is a hard hit that sends the ball directly downward over the top of the net into the opponents' court. The spike is made with an open hand, with a quick whip action of the shoulder, arm, and hand.

4. *Blocking:*   The block is a defensive skill used against a spiked ball. When an opponent is spiking, the blocker jumps, straightening the arms and reaching high above the net. It is important to keep facing the net with thumbs together, and fingers pointing upward.

ACTIVITY: VOLLEYBALL SKILL DRILLS

Focus/ Knowledge Skill	Equipment Needed	Suggested Grade Levels
Volleyball skills of serving, setting, and bumping are practiced in a challenging and cooperative activity.	1 volleyball or trainer for every 2 students Wall targets, basketball baskets	Grades 4–8 Modifications for grade levels: Lower the net and use volleyball trainers or other modified balls for younger or less-skilled students

Success Notes These activities build the necessary skills to participate in volleyball and similar games. Students should be motivated through individual challenges designed to meet their skill levels.

MAKING IT WORK

Setting Challenges

Toss and Set: Toss the ball, set it once, and catch. Toss the ball, set it twice, and catch. Toss the ball, set it as many times in a row as possible.

Wall Set: Toss the ball against the wall, and then set it back against the wall. Try keeping the ball in motion, keeping it above head level. Repeat the activity using a "wall target" approximately 24″ × 24″.

Partner Set: Stand about 10 feet apart and set the ball back and forth. At first, catch and toss, then move to continuous sets.

Basket Set:	Standing at the foul line, toss the ball and attempt to set it into the basket. After five attempts, rotate.
Agility Set:	Partners stand 10 feet apart, approximately 5 feet in front of a line. The pair volley the ball back and forth. After each set, students turn, run to the line behind them, and return to set again.
Back Set:	Partners stand 5 feet apart, facing the same direction. Player A tosses the ball and sets it back to player B who catches the ball, both players turn, and player B makes the back set. Try this in groups of three. With the middle player, C turning after each back set is made. In this variation, players should attempt to make continuous sets.

Bumping Challenges

Toss and Bump:	Toss the ball, bump the ball off the forearms, and catch. Toss the ball, bump it twice, and catch. Toss the ball and bump it as many times in a row as possible. Toss the ball, bump it, let it hit the ground, and bump again.
Wall Bump:	Toss the ball above your head, bump it into the wall, and catch it and try again. Repeat this activity using a wall target approximately 24″ × 24″.
Partner Bump:	Partners standing 10 feet apart toss, bump, and catch. Repeat the activity, having the receiving player kneeling. Toss the ball to the side of the receiving player so that she or he must move into proper position to make the bump.
Shuttle Bump:	Groups of four stand in a line, facing a wall. The first player tosses and bumps the ball into the wall, then quickly moves to the side and to the back of the line. The next player receives the rebound and, without catching the ball, bumps it back. This rotation continues as long as possible. If the ball hits the ground, the next player in line begins by tossing and bumping.

Serving Challenges (*underhand or overhand*)

Wall Serve:	Standing 10 feet away from a wall, serve the ball into the wall so that it hits the wall above a line 9 feet from the floor. After ten successful tries, move back 5 feet and try again.
Partner Serve:	Serve the ball over the net to a partner. Begin by standing 10 feet back from the net and moving back until reaching the service line.
Target Serve:	Place a hula hoop 10 feet back from the net. Serve the ball into the hoop. Begin standing 10 feet back from the net and moving back toward the service line after successful attempts.

Lane Serve: Divide each half of the court into four lanes. Divide the class into two equal groups standing on the service line on one side of the court. Each group should have four balls. On the "go "signal, the player in the right corner begins to serve one ball to each lane. Other players act as retrievers who get the balls and roll them back under the net to the opposite side. A player who has had four attempts moves to the end of the line.

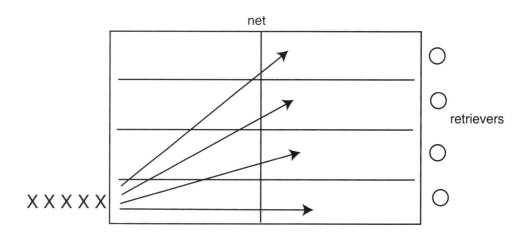

Blocking

Jump and Reach: Players jump vertically, keeping their bodies facing the net. As they jump, their arms thrust up, stretching overhead with palms facing the net.

Jump and Touch: Players make lines on opposite sides of the net facing a partner. On the "go" signal, players begin jumping as high as possible, trying to touch the fingertips of the person opposite them. After four jumps, everyone rotates one position to the right, with the end players moving around to the opposite line. Repeat until everyone is back in him or her starting position.

Note: If a player cannot jump high enough to touch the partner, have him or her concentrate on using proper form.

ACTIVITY: FOUR-SQUARE VOLLEYBALL—LOW NET

Focus/ Knowledge Skill	Equipment Needed	Suggested Grade Levels
Skills of setting, bumping, and team play are stressed.	4 pickleball nets and standards (construction/ caution tape also works well) Beachballs, volleyball trainers, or volleyballs	Grades 5–8 Modifications for grade levels: Have grade 5 students play with beachballs, moving up to trainers, and then regular volleyballs as students progress in ability. The height of the net may be raised as ability levels increase.

Success Notes Keep the game moving fast by not keeping score. Have students count the number of passes to different squares before the ball hits the ground. Remember that the object is to work on skill development.

MAKING IT WORK

Using pickleball nets and standards, arrange enough courts to allow all students to be involved at the same time. Organize the class into teams of two or three players each. Place one team in each of the four courts.

A player puts the ball into play with a serve from one court; the serve may go to any of the other three courts. After the serve, the play follows regular volleyball rules regarding the number of hits per side and no person being able to hit the ball twice in a row. If a team fails to return a hit to their court, the ball is picked up and put into play by that team.

Modifications:

• For more-skilled players, begin to play this game more like regular volleyball. The serve must come from behind the back line of the serving team. If a team fails to return a hit, the ball is given back to the serving team for their next serve. Score would be kept as in regular volleyball.

• As ability increases, begin to place two balls in play. Begin with beachballs and progress to trainers. This modification develops concentration and court awareness.

ACTIVITY: TARGET-SET RELAY

Focus/ Knowledge Skill	Equipment Needed	Suggested Grade Levels
Refinement of setting skills, hand-eye coordination, cooperation, and teamwork	Volleyballs, trainers, Nerfs™— 4 balls per team	Grades 5–8 Modifications for grade levels: Vary the distance from the target based on the ability of students.

Success Notes Stress tossing the ball directly overhead and use a good set with proper upward motion. Students should be encouraged to keep track of their teams' balls.

MAKING IT WORK

Place a large box, a ball cart, or four folding mats in a square (it works best if they are opened in A-frame fashion) in the center of the playing area. Place a series of cones approximately 10 feet from the target. Have students stand behind a cone in groups of four and face the target. Give each group a ball for each player. On the "go" signal, students begin to toss the ball up, set it, and try to get it into the center target. If the ball misses the target, the student retrieves it and goes to the end of the line. Play continues until each group has two balls in the center target. (If one or two groups get theirs in quickly, let the other keep going, and challenge the "winning" group to get all for balls in.)

Modifications:

- Challenge the groups to get all four balls in the target.

- Set a time limit—1 minute—and see how many balls each group can get in the target.

- Have students rotate groups. If a shot is missed, retrieve the ball and move one group to the right.

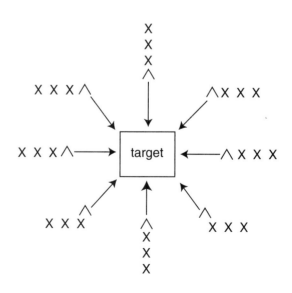

ACTIVITY: THREE-ON-THREE VOLLEYBALL

Focus/ Knowledge Skill	Equipment Needed	Suggested Grade Levels
Practice skills of setting, bumping, and serving, along with enhancement of communication and teaming skills.	Volleyball, volleyball trainer, or beachball Volleyball stands or net or tape Cone markers	Grades 6–8 Modifications for grade levels: Lower net or tape height depending on student's size and ability. Determine the type of ball to be used, depending on student ability (beachball 6, trainer 7, volleyball 8).

Success Notes Shorten the length of the court to approximately 10 to 15 feet on either side of the net or tape. Lower the height of the net to a level where the average person in the class can jump and touch the top. Have players on the side pass a ball over their heads while waiting; see how many round trips it can make during a game.

MAKING IT WORK

Line teams of any number up on the sidelines on both sides of the court. The first three from each side come out and begin play with a "friendly" serve from one team. A "friendly" serve can be either underhand or overhand, depending on abilities. However, the opponent must be able to hit it back, there can be no "aces." Play continues until one team makes a mistake allowing the ball to either hit the ground or go out of the court area. When a team makes a mistake, the next three players on both sides come in, and the players leaving the court run one lap and return to the end of their line.

Communication between team members is essential; they must "call" for the ball, cover an open space, back up, and encourage one another.

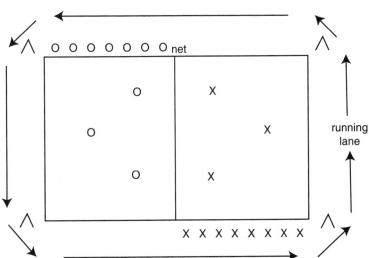

159

ACTIVITY: ROTATION VOLLEYBALL

Focus/ Knowledge Skill	Equipment Needed	Suggested Grade Levels
Volleyball skills of serving, setting, and bumping are practiced in a challenging and cooperative team activity.	1 volleyball, court, and net for each group of 12 students	Grades 6–8 Modifications for grade levels: Lower the net and use volleyball trainers or other modified balls for younger or less-skilled students.

Success Notes This activity requires previous knowledge of appropriate rotation patterns. Students should practice rotating and cooperating with one another before playing this game.

MAKING IT WORK

Divide the class into teams of six and assign two teams to each court. Play begins when one team (A) serves; when the ball makes it over the net the other team (B) attempts to return it. As team A serves, all members rotate one position (use normal rotation pattern). When team B returns the serve, they rotate. Play continues, with players rotating each time the ball clears the net until the ball fails to be returned.

Regulation volleyball rules apply, and score is kept as in a regulation game. However, to stress proper rotation and cooperation among team members, bonus points may be awarded (1 point for each proper rotation—actual score plus bonus points determine winners).

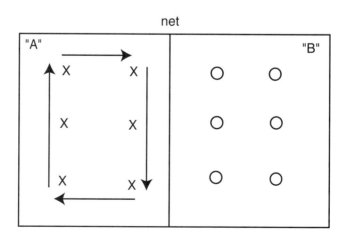

ACTIVITY: HOOP-TARGET VOLLEYBALL

Focus/ Knowledge Skill	Equipment Needed	Suggested Grade Levels
Volleyball skills of serving, setting, bumping, and spiking are practiced in a challenging activity.	1 volleyball, court, and net for each group of 12 students 4 hula hoops and heavy string/rope for each court	Grades 5–8 Modifications for grade levels: Use volleyball trainers or other modified balls for younger or less-skilled students.

Success Notes Stress team play, with backcourt players setting the ball to players closer to the net. The height of the hoop should be set at approximately extended-reach level of students.

MAKING IT WORK

Set up each court with four hula hoops suspended between two volleyball standards as shown in the diagram. Divide students into groups of approximately six, and assign two teams to each court.

Play begins with a backcourt player setting the ball to a front-row player, who hits the ball through a hoop. Prior to returning the "serve," the receiving team must contact the ball a minimum of two times before attempting a return through a hoop.

This pattern continues until the ball fails to be returned. Score is kept as in regular volleyball.

Modification:

Allow the ball to be returned without going through a hoop, but passing over the top of the hoops instead. To play this modification, score is kept by awarding 2 points each time a team returns the ball through a hoop and 1 point for returning it over the hoops. This game is played to 40 points.

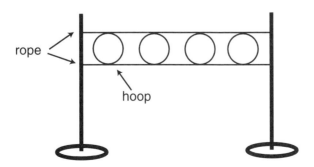

ACTIVITY: ALTERNATIVE-STATION VOLLEYBALL

Focus/ Knowledge Skill	Equipment Needed	Suggested Grade Levels
Volleyball skills of serving, setting, and bumping are practiced using a variety of equipment in a challenging format.	Volleyballs, volleyball trainers, Ball-Netos®, Volleybirds® Task cards for each station	Grades 4–8 Modifications for grade levels: Vary the activity and expectation level to meet class ability level.

Success Notes As volleyball involves hand-eye coordination, the stations used in this activity can easily be combined with juggling to increase student motivation.

MAKING IT WORK

After teaching the basic volleyball skills and reviewing the concept of proper positioning in relationship to the ball, divide the class into groups, and assign each to a station. As each station is a game or activity in itself, students should spend approximately 10 minutes at each station before rotating.

Sample Stations

Station 1—Volleybird: Groups of four, two on each side of a 5-foot net. Volley the Volleybird back and forth over the net.

Challenge—How many consecutive volleys can the group make?

Station 2—Bounce: Groups of four, two on each side of a 6-foot net. Using a volleyball trainer, volley back and forth, allowing one bounce on a side before the return.

Challenge—Pass the ball at least one time after the bounce before returning it over the net.

Station 3—Ball-Neto: Partners, each with a net and one ball for the pair, stand 10 feet apart passing the ball back and forth. Catches should be overhead, low, and chest high. In all cases, body position in relation to the ball should be stressed.

Challenge—Can you turn your back and catch? How many consecutive volleys can you make?

Note: A small towel can be used instead of a Ball-Neto.

Station 4—Partner Set: Groups of four, in file formation, face a wall. On the "go" signal, the first person in line sets the ball into the wall and quickly moves to the right, then to the end of the line. The next person moves up, receives the set, and returns it into the wall. This rotation continues until the ball is not returned to the wall.

Challenge—Can the groups rotate 10 times without a miss? Add in bumps.

Station 5—Serve/Set: Groups of four, two on each side of a 6-foot net. A person on one team begins with a serve. The receiving team attempts to set and return it over the net. If successful, players rotate and the receiving team becomes the serving team.

Challenge—Can your team rotate after each hit?

Sample Station Set-Up

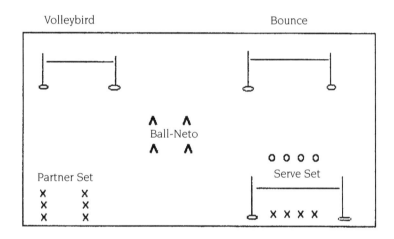

ACTIVITY: CRAZY BALL

Focus/ Knowledge Skill	Equipment Needed	Suggested Grade Levels
Setting accuracy and body position to receive and return balls.	7–9 volleyballs per court	Grades 6–8 Modifications for grade levels: Use volleyball trainers and lower net height for younger students.

Success Notes Remind students always to be alert and to stay in their positions so as not to interfere with teammates.

MAKING IT WORK

Divide the class into groups of six to eight students each, and assign each team to one side of a court. Give one team 4 (3) balls and the other 5 (4). On the "go" signal, players holding the ball toss and set it over the net. The receiving team sets the balls back. If a ball hits the ground or goes out-of-bounds, it may be put back in play by tossing and setting.

At the end of 3 minutes, play is stopped, and the number of balls on each side are counted. Teams change sides (keeping balls they have), and play is resumed. At the end of the second 3-minute period, the balls on each side are added to the first-period score. The team with the lower score wins.

Note: Have players look for open areas on the opponents' court to place the ball into. They may also pass the ball to other teammates before sending it over the net.

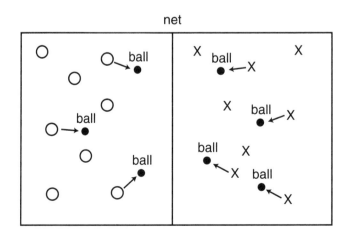

ACTIVITY: LEADER OF THE COURT

Focus/ Knowledge Skill	Equipment Needed	Suggested Grade Levels
Volleyball skills of serving, setting, and bumping are practiced in a challenging and cooperative team activity.	1 volleyball, court, and net for each group of 12 students	Grades 6–8 Modifications for grade levels: Lower the net and use volleyball trainers or other modified balls for younger or less-skilled students.

Success Notes Movement to the ball, proper body position in relation to the ball, and teamwork are stressed in this activity. Divide the court into sections if players are having difficulty in covering a position.

MAKING IT WORK

Divide the class into teams of six and assign two teams to each court. Two players from each team come onto the court to begin play. To begin the game, one team serves, and the player on the team receiving the serve must set it to the teammate, who may either send it over the net or make a second set to the partner. The volley continues until one team fails to return the ball.

The winning team stays on the court, and the other team sends two new players in. Once a pair has won 3 games, they also rotate out.

165

ACTIVITY: TEAM PASS

Focus/ Knowledge Skill	Equipment Needed	Suggested Grade Levels
Volleyball skills of setting, bumping, and receiving are practiced in a challenging and cooperative team activity.	1 volleyball, court, and net for each group of 16 students	Grades 7–8 Modifications for grade levels: Lower the net and use volleyball trainers or other modified balls for younger or less-skilled students.

Success Notes Prior practice, using simplified skill drills in setting, bumping, and receiving, will help students gain confidence and ability to successfully participate in this activity.

MAKING IT WORK

Divide students into groups of eight and assign two groups of eight to each court. At each court, the groups arrange themselves so that four players from each team are on each side of the net.

To begin, the end player on one team tosses the ball to the opposite teammate, who sets to the next teammate diagonally. This zigzag pattern continues down the line until it either touches the ground, is hit by a player other than the one being passed to, or has been successfully received and passed by all players. If the group is successful or makes a mistake, players from the next team move to the net.

Each successful pass is scored 1 point. Bonus points can be awarded for a "clean" run down the line.

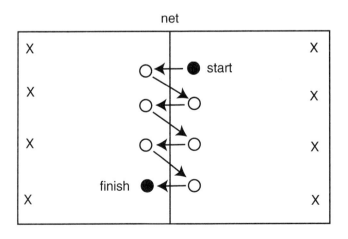

ACTIVITY: BACKBOARD SET

Focus/ Knowledge Skill	Equipment Needed	Suggested Grade Levels
Volleyball skills of setting and bumping for accuracy, as well as receiving, are combined in a cooperative group activity.	1 volleyball and basketball backboard for each group of 4–5 players	Grades 6–8 Modifications: Younger and less-skilled students should use volleyball trainers or Soft-Spike® balls.

Success Notes Prior to participating in this activity, students should have practiced bumping and setting skills with partners and against a wall.

MAKING IT WORK

Divide the class into groups of five, each assigned to a basketball backboard. Each group stands in a single line, facing the backboard from the foul line.

To begin, the first player from each line stands with the ball under the backboard, tosses the ball up, and sets it to the first player in line. This player makes a high set or bump in an attempt to hit the backboard, and catches the rebound. In turn, each player in line receives a volley from the baseline and attempts a set or bump into the backboard.

One point is awarded to the group for each set or bump that hits the backboard. Two points can be awarded if a basket is made.

Variation:

After the first hit into the backboard have the player receive the rebound and attempt another set or bump into the backboard. Players continue until they fail to hit the backboard or have returned 10 successfully.

ACTIVITY: VOLLEYBALL ACTIVITIES FOR SPECIAL NEEDS STUDENTS

Focus/ Knowledge Skill	Equipment Needed	Suggested Grade Levels
Eye-hand coordination skills through volleyball skill modifications for sets, spikes, bumps, and serves	Balloons, beachballs, volleyball trainers, foam balls All equipment should vary in size and color.	Grades 4–8

Success Notes A variety of experiences should be provided, with enough repetition at each developmental level to increase skill. Using student buddies working as partners, or having special needs students working as a part of a small group, provides positive reinforcement of learned skills and a "safety net" for students.

MAKING IT WORK

Note: Providing developmentally appropriate activities for students will depend on their individual needs. Care must be taken to determine the appropriate activities and instructional formats that best meet individual abilities and needs. The following activities have proven effective.

Instructional Progression

Balloon Play: Practice hitting the balloon with different body parts—hands, fingers, head, knees, toes, elbows, nose, shoulders, and backs of hands. Following the exploration, hit the balloon in an ordered pattern—hand to head to knee. After successful progressions are completed, introduce specific volleyball skills—set, bump, serve, and spike.

Beachball: Repeat progressive activities and exploration used with the balloon. Follow these activities by practicing sets, bumps, and serves with a partner or in a small group. When tossing the beachball, buddies should hold the ball where it can easily be seen. Also, it should be tossed from a short distance.

Volleyball Trainers: If appropriate, repeat the above activities using a volleyball trainer, Soft-Spike trainer, or foam ball.

Games and Drills

Special needs students can successfully participate in most lead-up games with some simple modifications.

General Modifications:

1. Use a beachball or other light and colorful ball. Special needs students should play in a specific area with a buddy. When the ball is hit in that area, the buddy can catch it, hold the ball, and have the partner hit it from her or his hand.

2. Play games in which the ball can bounce before it is hit. Special needs students may catch it and move forward before attempting a return. Returns can also be made by throwing the ball.

CLEAN UP YOUR COURT

Place six beach balls in each court. On the "go" signal, students begin hitting the balls over the net. Special needs students may catch and throw the ball. **Note:** This is a good game to teach awareness and movement to the ball while playing an area.

SECTION 4

Games That Teach

Interdisciplinary Instruction

- **R**einforce classroom concepts in combination with a physical activity.

- **E**nhance student learning and retention of knowledge and skill.

- **E**nhance building staff's cooperation and promote quality physical education as an integral part of the total educational process.

Games That Teach

- ✔ Modified Orienteering
- ✔ Action-Reaction
- ✔ Puzzle Relays
- ✔ Addition Robbery
- ✔ Basketball Multiplication
- ✔ Name That State
- ✔ Spot-Shot Math
- ✔ Bowling Math
- ✔ Cooperative Golf
- ✔ Predictions—Individual and Team
- ✔ Cooperative Challenges
- ✔ Cooperative Throwing and Catching
- ✔ Making a Difference
- ✔ Hit It—Name It
- ✔ Knowledge Tag
- ✔ Pyramid Relay
- ✔ Gee, I Can Do It at Home

Educators at all levels have discovered the benefits of integrating knowledge from various disciplines with movement and activity programs. This approach lessens curriculum fragmentation and enhances retention and use of knowledge as one subject in reinforced in other classes. Activities presented in Section 4 provide an approach that places emphasis on physical skill development while reinforcing knowledge in mathematics, social studies, health, science, and social skills. Use your imagination and create meaningful linkages.

ACTIVITY: MODIFIED ORIENTEERING

Focus/ Knowledge Skill	Equipment Needed	Suggested Grade Levels
The modifications of this challenging activity provide enhancements in the areas of geography, environmental studies, mathematics, and thinking and cooperation skills.	1 compass for each group of 2–3 students 3 × 5 cards, pencils for each group General map of the areas to be covered Cone markers	Grades 5–8

Success Notes Students must learn the basics of using a compass prior to going on a field experience. Even when doing this activity with older students, begin with the simpler tasks, moving students to the more demanding activities after they master the previous set.

MAKING IT WORK

Using the Compass: Arrange students in groups of two or three; give each group a compass, a 3 × 5 card, and a pencil. Begin by having the students find North. Once it is found, place a cone at a point approximately 25 yards from the students. Number an additional set of eight cones and place them in different locations approximately 25 yards from the center of the playing area. Explain to the class that North will always remain a constant, and the other compass readings can be taken based on their relationship to North. Ask students to write down the compass headings from the center of the playing area to each of the other cones. Have the students discuss how the readings were taken and compare answers.

First Course Trial: On an open playing field, mark and number (use large numbers that can be seen from a distance) twelve different locations at varying distances from the center. On 3 × 5 cards, write the numbers 1–12, in a different sequence on each card. Give one card and pencil to each group of two or three students. Beginning in the center of the area, students locate the first numbered cone on their cards, record the compass heading, and run to it. From that cone they locate the next numbered cone, record the compass heading, and run to it. This sequence continues until they have recorded the compass heading to each cone in their sequence. The final listing should be from the last cone back to the center.

Second Course Trial: This field experience is similar to the first, with one major exception. Rather than writing the numbers of the cones down, write the compass heading from each group's sequence. The object is for the group to read the compass heading on the card, locate the cone, run to it, and write the cone number down on the card next to the heading.

320 degrees from center mark————————cone number ___(6)___

60 degrees from cone number ___(6)___ to cone number ___(4)___

128 degrees from cone number ___(4)___ to cone number ___(8)___

Third Course Trial: During this trial, students must locate marks that are not directly visible from any point. Using the 3 × 5 card format as in the second trail, locate marks behind trees or bushes, around the corner of a building, under a bench, and so on. As the students run to that area, they must also be looking for the mark. When it is found, they must write the number and describe the location of the mark.

320 degrees from center mark————————cone number ___(6—by pine tree)___

60 degrees from cone number ___(6)___ to cone number ___(4—under bench)___

128 degrees from cone number ___(4)___ to cone number ___(8—on oak tree)___

Fourth Course Trial: This is the most challenging trial. Students are provided maps of the area noting objects and general terrain. On the 3 × 5 card, list the compass headings to the marks. Get a little "fancy" this time; put marks on opposite sides of buildings or objects that students must go around and relocate their compass heading. Students mark their cards as in Trial 3.

Note: Remember to make the mark sequence listed on each card different. This keeps groups from simply following one another. For more advanced students, give each group a stopwatch, and have them record their running time between marks; add the times to determine the total running time for each group to complete the course.

ACTIVITY: ACTION-REACTION

Focus/ Knowledge Skill	Equipment Needed	Suggested Grade Levels
The action of the body directly affects the action of an object that is thrown or struck. Spinning action of a ball in flight will be directly related to how it was thrown or struck.	Whiffle balls, golf balls, tennis balls Plastic bats, golf clubs, pickleball paddles, and tennis rackets	Grades 7–8

Success Notes Demonstrate each action for the class prior to letting students experiment. Explain the importance of this knowledge in playing various sports; for example, a slice or hook in golf, a curve ball in baseball, a drop shot in tennis.

MAKING IT WORK

Discuss with students that the physical laws of nature tell us that for every action there is an equal and opposite reaction. This applies to throwing or striking a ball during many physical activities.

Baseball: When a batted ball is hit on the lower half of the bat, it will have back spin, causing it to go up and to the rear. Demonstrate by taking a whiffle ball and striking it with your hand on the bottom, moving forward. Which way does it spin?

When throwing a ball, if you use a throwing motion that puts a right-hand spin on the ball it will curve to the right; left-hand spin will curve to the left. Demonstrate by taking a ball, placing it on the floor, and rolling it with a spinning motion; watch it curve.

Golf: When a ball is hit with a right-hand spin (clockwise) it will slice, turn to the right; left-hand spin will hook the ball, turn to the left. These actions are caused by the way the club head makes contact with the ball. Show that an "outside-in" swing will put a clockwise spin and cause a slice, and an "inside-out" swing will put counterclockwise pins on it and cause a hook.

Racket Sports: The position of the racket face can be compared to the palm of the hand making contact with the ball if the player were not holding a racket. The direction in which the racket face is moving is the direction of flight the ball will take. If the racket face is "closed," the ball will go the left for a right-handed player. If the racket comes over the top of the ball, putting top spin on, the ball will go downward. **175**

Demonstrate by striking a ball slowly with the hand and watching the direction in which the ball travels.

Bowling: If you put a clockwise spin on the ball, it will curve to the right; a counterclockwise spin will curve to the left. Demonstrate by rolling a bowling ball approximately 25 feet with different spins. Ask students what spare combinations would require different spins to complete.

After providing several demonstrations, give the students an opportunity to practice some of the action-reaction experiments. As you move about the room, ask what other activities students can think of that will demonstrate this concept.

Students can demonstrate their knowledge by making a class presentation and demonstrating the effects of motion on an object.

ACTIVITY: PUZZLE RELAYS

Focus/ Knowledge Skill	Equipment Needed	Suggested Grade Levels
Reinforce basic knowledge regarding health, geography, spelling, or math while performing various physical activities.	Puzzle sets equal to the number of relay teams participating 1 hula hoop for each team Jump ropes, balls, etc., depending on the physical activity	Grades 4–7 Modifications for grade levels: Check with either the clas room or subject-area teacher to see what knowledge to reinforce.

Success Notes When cutting the puzzle pieces, keep them challenging yet easy enough to allow students to be successful.

MAKING IT WORK

Divide students into group of five. Have them stand in a relay line behind a poly-spot at one end of the playing area. At the other end, place the puzzle pieces for each team in a hula hoop; each team should have a different puzzle but with an equal number of pieces. On the "go" signal, the first student runs to get one puzzle piece, comes back to the group, puts the puzzle piece in the hoop, performs the designated activity, and touches the hand of the next person. This rotation continues until all puzzle pieces are brought back.

When the last puzzle piece is back, the group begins to put the pieces together. After the puzzle is together, the group sits until all other groups are finished. After all puzzles are put together, the pieces are returned to the other end and placed in the hula hoop. Each team then moves one station to the right. This rotation continues until each group has solved each puzzle. At the conclusion of the activity, ask students to discuss the specifics of each puzzle.

Example: Physical Activity—After running down and bringing back a puzzle piece, jump rope 20 times; bounce a basketball 20 times; do a "self-set" with a volleyball 10 times; figure 8 dribble with a soccer ball.

Puzzle Concepts—Names of countries, spelling words, fitness concepts, math facts.

SPAIN   FLEXIBILITY $24 \times 15 = 360$

Puzzle Relay Samples

Note: When making puzzles for class use, each should be done on large poster board and laminated.

HEALTH CONCEPTS:

REDUCE STRESS   CARDIOVASCULAR   DURATION
RESTING HEART RATE   MUSCULAR STRENGTH   ENDURANCE
BODY COMPOSITION   LEAN MASS   FAT MASS
TARGET HEART RATE   MAXIMUM HEART RATE   OXYGEN

OTHER CONCEPTS:

COUNTRIES   STATES   CAPITALS
MAJOR CITIES   CURRENT EVENTS   PRESIDENTS
HISTORY FACTS   MATH FACTS   ART

MAKING PUZZLES:

Cut puzzles in various shapes making it a challenge (not too difficult) for students to assemble them.

ACTIVITY: ADDITION ROBBERY

Focus/ Knowledge Skill	Equipment Needed	Suggested Grade Levels
Agility and cooperative learning; review and practice of addition and subtraction	8 beanbags 7 tennis balls 3 volleyballs 5 softballs 10 hockey pucks 5 frisbees 2 footballs 4 hula hoops Other equipment may be substituted, depending on your inventory.	Grades 4–7

Success Notes When placing the hula hoops in each corner, make sure that they are equal distances from the center and one another. This creates equal running distances for each team. Let students know that they must keep adding or subtracting when each team is placed in or taken out of their hoop.

MAKING IT WORK

Place 1 hula hoop in each corner of a basketball court. Have students make equal groups, facing the center, behind each hoop. In the center of the gym place different objects. Each object should be assigned a different number value.

Objects:	Point Value	Number in Center
Beanbags	3	8
Tennis Balls	5	7
Volleyballs	12	3
Softballs	7	5
Hockey Pucks	2	10
Frisbees	8	5
Footballs	15	2

Using a relay format, each team sends students to the center to get an object and bring it back to their hoop. When one person returns, the next one goes to the center and brings back another object. When all objects are gone from the center, players may go to another group's hoop and take one of their objects (players may not guard their objects). Play continues until one team gets objects in their hoop totaling 30 or more points.

179

Modifications:

Use only beanbags, giving each color a different value. Change the total necessary to win or number of various objects available, making the game go more quickly or more slowly.

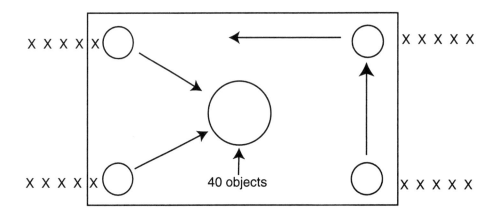

ACTIVITY: BASKETBALL MULTIPLICATION

Focus/ Knowledge Skill	Equipment Needed	Suggested Grade Levels
Basketball skill development;	2 basket balls for each basket math facts Hula hoops or poly-spots Score cards and pencils	Grades 4–7 Modifications for grade levels: Use adjustable basket heights, with grade 4 students playing on an 8-foot hoop, grade 5 on a 9-foot hoop, and grades 6 and 7 on a 10-foot hoop. Use appropriate math facts for ability of students.

Success Notes Use math facts at an appropriate level so that all students can achieve success. If some students have problems, let them work in cooperative groups.

MAKING IT WORK

Place hula hoops or poly-spots at various distances from each basket. Tape a number on each hoop or spot. Also assign a number to each basket. Give each student a piece of paper and pencil and ask them to divide themselves into equal groups at each basket.

On signal, students being shooting from the various hoop and spot locations. If a shot is made they multiply the number on the hoop or spot by the number assigned to the basket. They then write the answer on the score card. After 3 minutes, they add the numbers, record the sum, and rotate to the next basket. Students continue rotating until all baskets have been played. After playing all baskets, students should add the total of all scores.

Modifications:
Play as a team of two or four, using one score card.
Use other mathematical operations as appropriate for the grade level and ability of students.

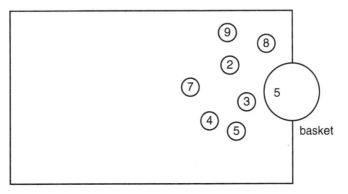

ACTIVITY: NAME THAT STATE

Focus/ Knowledge Skill	Equipment Needed	Suggested Grade Levels
Various skill development activities through the use of relay variations; refinement of various locomotor skills; reinforcement of states, capitals, major cities	Set of letter flash cards for each group A–Z, with double letters for each vowel and S, T, R, L, H, and N 2 cone markers for each group 2 hula hoops for each group Balls, depending on skill development focus	Grades 4–5 Modifications: Skill tasks can be varied, depending on the unit focus. *volleyball—self volley *basketball—dribble the ball while moving to opposite end *soccer—dribble and shoot

Success Notes Check with the classroom or social studies teacher to determine the focus of the relay. If students are just beginning to learn the material to be used, post a chart with capitals, states, and countries on a wall. Let them know that they may send one student from their group to the chart to check answers.

MAKING IT WORK

Have students get into equal groups, each sitting around a hoop/cone at one end of the gym. Each group should have a complete set of letter cards and any equipment to be used.

To begin, give the students a movement challenge; e.g., all jump rope ten times, volley a volleyball between members of your group 4 times, do a basketball chest pass to each member of your group 3 times. After giving them the movement challenge ask them to spell a specific state, capital, country, etc. On the "go" signal, students complete the movement task, then work together to determine how to spell the answer, pick up cards and run to the hoop at the opposite end and spell the word, and run back to their original starting position.

Every group with the correct answer gets one point.

Modifications

Give such tasks as:

- States with six letters in their names (Kansas, Hawaii, Nevada, Oregon)
- Capitals with six letters in their names (Denver, St. Paul, Pierre, Helena)
- States that begin with a vowel (Alabama, Ohio, Illinois)
- Complete a sentence: The capital of Washington is? (Olympia)

ACTIVITY: SPOT-SHOT MATH

Focus/ Knowledge Skill	Equipment Needed	Suggested Grade Levels
Basketball skills of shooting from various locations; various mathematical operations	2 or 3 basketballs for each basket Poly-spots or cones "Math-Fact" cards Score cards and pencils	Grades 4–8 Modifications for grade levels: Use adjustable basket heights, with grade 4 students playing on an 8-foot hoop, grade 5 on a 9-foot hoop, and grades 6–8 on a 10-foot hoop. Mathematical operations and problems should be appropriate for each grade level.

Success Notes Do not place emphasis on winning. Have students achieve success from shooting baskets and solving math problems.

MAKING IT WORK

At each available basket place poly-spots or cones are varying distances from the hoop. Each spot or cone should have a "Math-Fact" card taped to it. Each basket should have a different mathematical operation; for example, Basket 1, addition; Basket 2, multiplication; Basket 3, subtraction; Basket 4, division. Give each student a "Spot-Shot Math" score card, and have them all go to a basket.

On signal, students begin shooting baskets from each spot at the assigned basket. When a basket is made, they record the math problem and the answer, turn over the "Math-Fact" card and check the answer. Students keep shooting at this basket for 3 minutes. After time has expired, they rotate to the next basket and begin again. After shooting at each basket, students add the total of all answered to see who has the highest total.

Modifications:

Play as teams of two or 4 using one score card.

Have more advanced players subtract 2 for every missed shot.

Front Side

$$\begin{array}{r} 9 \\ \times\, 4 \\ \hline \end{array}$$

Back Side

$$\begin{array}{r} 9 \\ \times\, 4 \\ \hline 36 \end{array}$$

ACTIVITY: BOWLING MATH

Focus/ Knowledge Skill	Equipment Needed	Suggested Grade Levels
Reinforce math skills while practicing bowling technique.	1 bowling lane for each group "Bowling Math" score card and pencil for each student	Grades 4–8 Modifications for grade levels: Math concepts should be appropriate for the class.

Success Notes Allow students to work in groups to answer math questions.

MAKING IT WORK

This is an excellent activity to use while practicing bowling skills. Unlike the regulation bowling, students get two rolls each frame (even if they get a strike on the first roll). To score, students add the total number of pins knocked down in the frame and do the calculation listed for that frame to determine their score. After 10 frames, the totals are added to get the final score.

BOWLING MATH SCORE CARD:

PLAYER: _____

FRAME 1	_____ PINS	+ 13 = _____
FRAME 2	_____ PINS	× 9 = _____
FRAME 3	_____ PINS	+ 21 = _____
FRAME 4	_____ PINS	− 9 = _____
FRAME 5	_____ PINS	× 18 = _____
FRAME 6	_____ PINS	− 12 = _____
FRAME 7	_____ PINS	+ 19 = _____
FRAME 8	_____ PINS	× 8 = _____
FRAME 9	_____ PINS	− 8 = _____
FRAME 10	_____ PINS	+ 29 = _____
	TOTAL	_____

ACTIVITY: COOPERATIVE GOLF

Focus/ Knowledge Skill	Equipment Needed	Suggested Grade Levels
Physical skills of chipping, hitting, and catching—along with cooperation, thinking skills, and communication—are practiced.	9 + poly-spots or cone markers 9 hula hoops A whiffle ball and club for each pair of students—use tennis balls for variety Score card and pencil	Grades 4–7 Modifications for grade levels: Use balls appropriate to skills that have been previously taught Frisbees provide a real challenge.

Success Notes Before starting the activity, give students the challenge to design the course. Have them use a poly-spot for the tee, hula hoops for cups, and cones or poly-spots for hazards. Lay colored construction tape on the group to make hole boundaries.

MAKING IT WORK

Assign students, in pairs, to a starting hole. To begin, one student stands at the tee and hits the ball to the partner, who has run down the hole. If the ball is caught, the partner who hit the ball runs past the partner to catch the next hit. This rotation continues until a player stands in the hoop and catches the ball. The group's score is the total number of throws made to get the ball into the hoop.

If a ball is dropped, it should be picked up and moved back 5 steps from where the receiver was standing. One additional point is added to the pairs score for the hole. After they finish the hole, they go to the next tee area.

After completing all nine holes, the group should complete the following tasks:

- Add their total score for nine holes.
- Average the score for nine holes to see what their hole average was.
- Average the total scores for the class.

SAMPLE SCORE CARD

Player	1	2	3	4	5	6	7	8	9	Total

Team Total _____   Team Average: _____   **185**

| Fitness Activities | Skill Development | Games That Teach | Healthy Lifestyles | Keeping Track |

ACTIVITY: PREDICTIONS—INDIVIDUAL AND TEAM

Focus/ Knowledge Skill	Equipment Needed	Suggested Grade Levels
Mathematical and thinking skills involved in predicting outcomes and comparing them to actual scores are utilized while enhancing cardiovascular endurance, muscular strength, and activity skills.	Beanbags, jump ropes, volleyballs, hula hoops, and other equipment, depending on skill development focus Score cards and pencils	Grades 4–8 Modifications for grade levels: Use age-appropriate skills, and allow a longer time period for group discussions with younger students.

Success Notes Provide students with enough time to discuss, record, and calculate their scores before rotating. Assign students to groups where appropriate cooperative learning situations may be used; for example, student leaders can assist others with math skills.

MAKING IT WORK

Arrange six or more challenging stations around the gym. Have students get in groups of approximately five, and assign each group to a station. After the groups have been assigned, give each team a score card and pencil (if doing individual prediction, give each student a score card).

To begin, give a "ready" signal and allow students 30 to 45 seconds to discuss, predict, and write down what their results will be at that station. On the "go" signal, students do the activity for 3 minutes. After the 3 minutes of activity, students stop and record their actual score, and calculate the difference between their prediction and actual score. Continue until each group has completed all stations. At the conclusion, discuss with students the accuracy of their predictions.

Sample Stations
- **Push-Ups:** Using any variation, how many push-ups can the team, a pair, or an individual, do in 3 minutes? (Not all team members must go for the entire 3 minutes.)
- **Beanbag Pick-Up:** Place a large number of beanbags or other objects at one end of the gym. Have students line up in relay lines at the other end. Students run one at a time, take one beanbag, and return to the group. The task is to predict how many beanbags the team, or individual, will return in 3 minutes.
- **Curl-Ups:** How many curl-ups can the team, or individual, do in 3 minutes?

186

- **Ball Hop:** Putting a ball between their knees, students hop from one line to another. The task is to see how many round trips the team, or individual student, can make in 3 minutes. (If the ball drops, it must be picked up, and the student returns to the closest line already touched.)
- **Speed Jumps:** How many successful turns of a jump rope can the team, or individual, make in 3 minutes?
- **Volleyball Set:** Each team member is given a volleyball or trainer. The task is for each student to volley the ball overhead as many times as he or she can in 3 minutes. If the ball drops or is caught, the count resumes at the last successful number.

PREDICTION SCORE CARD

Team or Individual Name: _____

CHALLENGE	PREDICTION	ACTUAL	DIFFERENCE
PUSH-UP			
BEANBAG PICK-UP			
CURL-UP			
BALL HOP			
SPEED JUMP			
VOLLEYBALL SET			

ACTIVITY: COOPERATIVE CHALLENGES

Focus/ Knowledge Skill	Equipment Needed	Suggested Grade Levels
Various skills are utilized in attempting challenges. Communication and co-operative skills are enhanced through these activities.	Equipment needs will vary, depending on the stations used.	Grades 4–8 Modifications for grade levels: Vary the skills necessary to ensure safety and trust among students.

Success Notes When the first presenting these challenges, begin with partners or small groups. Prior to using a station approach, have all students attempt basic tasks. This helps to build the trust and cooperation necessary to work independently.

MAKING IT WORK

Sample Activities

A station approach may be used after students gain a feeling of trust and cooperation. The sample activities noted below provide for fun challenges along with skill development opportunities.

Ball Carry: Have students carry one or two balls from one side of the basketball court to the other without using their hands or forearms.

Milk-Crate Stand: See if the entire group can stand on a milk crate for 20 seconds.

Hula Hoop Pass: Have the group form a circle holding hands, with the hula hoop on the arm of one person. The group tries to pass the hoop around the circle without letting go of hands. Reverse direction on signal.

Launch and Catch: Blow up numerous balloons (do not tie the ends). Have one student hold the end while the partner is the "catcher." On signal, the holder lets go and the catcher attempts to catch it before it hits the ground.

Standing Partner Push-Up Balance: Two people face each other and place their palms together. Each person then takes one step backward at a time until they cannot support each other.

Car/Driver: Have one person blindfolded (car) and one person the "driver." The driver must steer the car around the room, either verbally or manually, without any collisions. For an additional challenge, place obstacles around the room.

Trust Fall:	Have one person be the "catcher" and one the "faller." Have the faller fall backward into the catchers hands. (Do this on a mat for safety, and assign students into groups by size and strength.)
Backward Get-Up:	This may be done with partners or in a group. Have students link arms while sitting back to back. On the "go" signal, have them simultaneously stand up and sit back down. (Start with partners and move to a group after they have experienced success.)
Forward Get-Up:	Repeat the Backward Get-Up, but have the students sit facing each other with hands joined.
Washing Machine:	Repeat the Trust Fall, but have the faller fall forwards (arms folded across the chest) to one person, and have that catcher push the faller backward to the next catcher. This activity can also be done by passing the person sideways around the group.

ACTIVITY: COOPERATIVE THROWING AND CATCHING

Focus/ Knowledge Skill	Equipment Needed	Suggested Grade Levels
Various throwing and catching skills are enhanced through cooperative challenges.	Footballs, tennis balls, whiffle balls, softballs, for each pair of students	Grades 4–6

Success Notes These challenging activities provide an opportunity to enhance throwing and catching skills in a cooperative format. While challenging the students, vary the tasks of individual groups to meet the skill and motivation levels of all students.

MAKING IT WORK

Challenges

Machine Gun: In groups of two, one person holding two balls. Toss two balls at a time to your partner. Try tossing different balls, tossing at different times, crossing, and so forth.

3 on 1 Toss: In groups of four, three players in a line, one 6 feet in front, two of the line players have one ball with the third holding two. The line players quickly, and in succession, toss one at a time to the front player. How many can the person catch? Add the four players' catches together for a team score.

Wrong Way: In groups of two, partners facing each other, one with a ball. On the "go" signal, the partner without the ball begins to jog backward away from the partner with the ball, about 10–15 feet. The partner with the ball calls "Ball" and tosses the ball in front of the partner. The catcher runs forward and tries to make the catch.

Fire Four: Using the same format as for "3 on 1," toss all four balls at the same time. Remember, this is a team cooperation activity. The goal is to see how many balls your team can catch. **Note:** Use fluff, yarn, or whiffle balls for this activity.

ACTIVITY: MAKING A DIFFERENCE

Focus/ Knowledge Skill	Equipment Needed	Suggested Grade Levels
Students conduct a parent and community survey, analyze results, make recommendations, and plan activities related to physical fitness.	Survey instrument Access to resource material related to the need for physical activity among the total population	Grades 7–8

Success Notes This is a great activity to combine with "Healthy Lifestyles" lessons related to goal setting and development of individual health and fitness plans.

MAKING IT WORK

Have students select, or be assigned, a survey/research partner. To begin, each group should research the benefits of physical activity and the goals established by the Centers for Disease Control, as related to physical activity patterns.

After conducting the basic research, class discussions should be held, related to personal and family activity patterns. Students then graph these patterns and draw conclusions—both positive and negative—and draft plans for areas needing improvement.

Having gained a base of knowledge, groups now go to the general school population, staff and students, and conduct the survey. To avoid duplication of data, each group should select specific classes or groups of students to survey. After the data are collected, groups analyze their data, combine with other groups, and create a school profile. Upon review of the profile, general conclusions are drawn, and recommendations for improvement are made.

Extension:

After the school profile has been analyzed and recommendations made, groups of students can work with others, staff and community members, to develop and implement a "Physical Activity" plan for the school; for example, an "activity" break time for all students and staff from 10:15 to 10:25 each day, bike-to-school day, activity homework groups.

PHYSICAL ACTIVITY SURVEY
(MAKING A DIFFERENCE)

Completing the Survey:
(Before asking questions, let the person know that this survey is a class project to determine the amount and type of physical activity students and adults participate in on a regular basis. The survey is anonymous, and the results will be used to see what improvements can be made, and how the class might help others to become more physically active.)

SURVEY

Student Grade Level: _____   **Gender:** _____

Adult Age: _____   **Gender:** _____

1. Do you participate in a regular exercise program?   YES   NO
    a. If YES, what activities do you do?

    b. If YES, how often do you participate?

    c. If NO, why not?

2. Are you physically active but do not participate in a regular exercise program?
    YES   NO
    a. What type of activity are you involved in? (mowing lawn, seasonal activities, etc.)

3. When participating in physical activity, are you alone or with others?
    ALONE   OTHERS
    a. If with others, are they: FRIENDS   FAMILY   OTHERS

4. Why is physical activity important to you?

5. If physical activity is not important to you, what is the reason?

6. Do you: Use tobacco (smoke or chew)   YES   NO
    Use alcohol or other drugs   YES   NO
    Get 8 hours of sleep each night?   YES   NO
    Walk as part of your regular day?   YES   NO
    Eat 3 regular meals per day?   YES   NO

7. Do you believe you are physically fit?   YES   NO

ACTIVITY: HIT IT—NAME IT

Focus/ Knowledge Skill	Equipment Needed	Suggested Grade Levels
Practice of throwing or racket sport skills in combination with learning geographical locations	1 tennis ball per group 1 large map for each group (maps should vary, depending on area of study)	Grades 4–6

Success Notes Work with classroom teachers regarding areas of emphasis and the construction of maps. Have students construct the maps as part of a geography project.

MAKING IT WORK

Place enlarged maps in various locations and heights around the gym. Place a throwing/hitting position at an appropriate distance from the target: throwing, 40 feet, pickleball or tennis, 25 feet. Also, place a small duplicate map and pencil at the station.

Divide students into groups, and assign to a map location. On the "go" signal, students begin throwing or hitting the ball toward the target. When hitting an area, the student should write the name on a duplicate map at the station. Students continue rotating until all map locations have been hit and named.

Example:

Map of the United States:	Hit a state, name it, and list capital city.
Map of North and South America:	Hit a country; name it.
Map of a State:	Hit major cities and geographical features, and name them.

ACTIVITY: KNOWLEDGE TAG

Focus/ Knowledge Skill	Equipment Needed	Suggested Grade Levels
This activity combines content basics from science, social studies, health, or other subject areas with a fast-moving tag game.	Knowledge Cards with answers. 3 or 4 foam frisbees or small balls	Grades 4–8 Modifications for grade levels: Work closely with others in getting "Knowledge Card" questions that are appropriate.

Success Notes This activity should be developed in consultation with other subject-area teachers. The questions placed on the Knowledge Cards should reinforce what is being taught at the time in other subjects.

MAKING IT WORK
In this variation of "freeze tag," students should find an open space within the boundaries of the basketball court. Designate three or four "taggers" and three or four "thawers." Give each tagger a foam frisbee or ball, and the thawers each a set of Knowledge Cards.

On the "go" signal, students begin the tag game. When tagged, the student stops and begins doing jumping jacks. The thawer's role is to find a student who has been tagged and ask that student a question. If the question is answered correctly, the student goes free; if answered incorrectly, she or he is given another question. If the second question is answered incorrectly, the student must go to the side and complete a "Challenge Task" before reentering the game.

Note: With lower-ability students—especially academically, allow the thawer to give hints or even change the question to something easier; for example, In what direction does the sun rise? What is the capital of this state?

SAMPLE PHYSICAL CHALLENGES

It is best to use activities that do not need equipment.

10 push-ups	25 skier's jumps over a line	10 Vertical jumps
15 crunches	Rub head and pat stomach 10 times	

SAMPLE KNOWLEDGE CARDS

Remember to ask other staff members for questions and answers related to areas that are being covered in their classes. This activity should help to reinforce academic knowledge.

Put on 3 × 5 Cards (Question and answer on the same side)

Who was called the "Father of the Constitution"?

JAMES MADISON

What do the initials "D.C." (which follow Washington) stand for?

DISTRICT OF COLUMBIA

What state did not send a delegate to the convention to revise the Articles of Confederation?

RHODE ISLAND

In what city would you find the Baseball Hall of Fame?

COOPERSTOWN, NEW YORK

The type of energy used to move things is called?

KINETIC ENERGY

| Fitness Activities | Skill Development | Games That Teach | Healthy Lifestyles | Keeping Track |

ACTIVITY: PYRAMID RELAY

Focus/ Knowledge Skill	Equipment Needed	Suggested Grade Levels
An exciting relay combining nutrition information with various running patterns	Food cards representing each component of the food pyramid 6 hula hoops 6 "Food Pyramid" charts	Grades 4–6 Modifications for grade levels: Change the running patterns for older classes; for example, run a zigzag course through cones, or dribble a basketball while running.

Success Notes Review the food pyramid with the class prior to beginning the activity. Place various posters or drawings of the pyramid in sight of each group.

MAKING IT WORK
Place six hula hoops at one end of the gym. At the opposite end, place six "Food Pyramid" charts. Have students, in groups of four to five, form a line behind the charts at one end, and place a set of food cards in each hoop at the opposite end. On the "go" signal, the first student in each line moves to the other end, gets a food card, returns, and places it in the correct category, in the pyramid. They continue until they have the correct number of servings per category.

After each group has completed its pyramid, have groups switch and check one another's work.

Variations:
1. Have the groups complete the pyramid for a person who can have no dairy products.
2. Plan the pyramid for a vegetarian.
3. Have students perform a different fitness activity after each category has been completed.
4. Complete one food category before changing to the next sections of the pyramid.

SAMPLE FOOD PYRAMID CHART

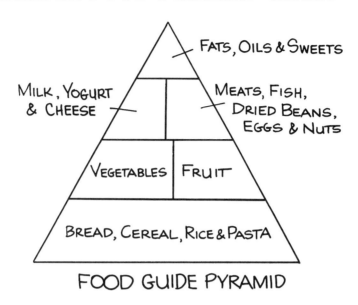

FOOD GUIDE PYRAMID

FOOD PYRAMID CATEGORIES AND SERVINGS
(Enlarge and place on 3 × 5 cards)

Breads, Cereals, Rice, and Pasta (6–11 servings)
- 1 slice of bread, 1/2 bagel, or 1/2 English muffin
- 1 small roll
- 1 ounce dry cereal
- 1/2 cup of cooked rice or pasta
- 3–4 small crackers

Vegetables (3–5 servings)
- 1 cup of leafy vegetables
- 1/2 cup of raw or cooked vegetables

Fruits (2–4 servings)
- 1 medium piece of fruit or melon wedge
- 1/2 cup of berries, grapefruit, or canned fruit

Milk, Yogurt, Cheese (2–3 servings)
- 1 cup of milk
- $1\frac{1}{2}$ ounces of cheese
- 2 ounces of processed cheese

Meat, Fish, Poultry, Dry Beans, Eggs, Nuts (2–3 servings)
- 2–3 ounces of cooked fish, poultry, or trimmed red meat
- 1–$1\frac{1}{2}$ cups of cooked dry beans
- 2–3 eggs
- 4–6 tablespoons of peanut butter
- 1 cup of peanuts

Fats, Oils, and Sugars (use sparingly 1–2 servings, depending on size)
- Condiments, except for mayonnaise, 1–2 tablespoons
- Salad dressings—regular, 1–2 tablespoons
- Cookies, candy bars, soda pop—depends upon the kind, but no more than 3–4 per week.

ACTIVITY: GEE, I CAN DO IT AT HOME

Focus/ Knowledge Skill	Equipment Needed	Suggested Grade Levels
Students gain an understanding of how a person can maintain an appropriate state of health-related fitness.	Articles and other resource materials that contain definitions and examples of health-related fitness. Individual "Home Fitness Program" work sheets	Grades 6–8

Success Notes Provide students with an introduction to health-related fitness components, and show them appropriate resources or direct them to where to find the resources.

MAKING IT WORK

Arrange students into groups of four or fewer, and have them begin to complete section 1 of the work sheet. When they are completing section 2, have them generate a listing of both traditional and nontraditional activities. When both sections have been completed, bring the group together, and ask each group to share and discuss the results of their research.

After completing the discussion, assign each individual the task to create a personal health-related fitness program to participate in for the next two weeks. Let them know that you will randomly be checking their work sheets, so they should bring them to class each day. Emphasize that it is important to be active each day and to record progress toward goals.

HOME FITNESS PROGRAM
WORK SHEET

Define the following terms according to your research.

1. Muscular Strength:_____

   _____

2. Flexibility: _____

   _____

3. Cardiovascular Endurance: _____

   _____

4. Body Composition (Lean/Fat Mass): _____

   _____

List activities that could be done at home without purchasing equipment.

1. Muscular Strength:
   (Example: Use 2 large family-size cans of soup as weights for arm curls, sitting press, etc.)

   _____

   _____

2. Flexibility:
   (Example: Stretch shoulders by standing in a doorway; clasp hands, turn palms up trying to reach the top without standing on tiptoes.)

   _____

   _____

3. Cardiovascular Endurance:
   (Example: Jog in place or outside for 10 minutes.)

   _____

   _____

4. Body Composition:
   (Example: Chart your diet for two days to see if you are meeting the Pyramid Guidelines.)

   _____

   _____

   _____

Fitness Progress Report

For the next two weeks, participate in a home fitness program at least three days a week. Use the four health-related components stated on the work sheet.

Component: Flexibility

Date	Activity	Body part/area this activity is designed to enhance	Length of participation or number of repetitions (min. 30 seconds or 10 repetitions)	Initial

Component: Muscular Strength

Date	Activity	Body part/area this activity is designed to enhance	Length of participation or number of repetitions (min. 30 seconds or 10 repetitions)	Initial

Component: **Body Composition**

Date	Activity	Benefit to your Diet	Long-Term Goal	Initial

Component: **Cardiovascular Endurance**

Date	Activity	Body part/area this activity is designed to enhance	Length of participation or number of repetitions (min. 30 seconds or 10 repetitions)	Initial

SECTION 5

Healthy Lifestyles

MAKING THE CONNECTION

- Assist students in developing a personal health, fitness, and activity plan.

- Provide a practical application of knowledge and skill taught in class.

- Promote carry-over of school activities to the home and community.

Healthy Lifestyles

Personal Goal Progress Log

✔ **Lifestyle Tag**

✔ **Personal Logs: Keeping Track of Your Healthy Lifestyle**

   ➤ Recreational Activity Log

   ➤ Being Flexible

   ➤ Daily Flexibility Log

   ➤ Activity Log

   ➤ How Did You Spend Your Time?

   ➤ Personal Goal Progress Log

   ➤ Weekly Aerobics Program

   ➤ Getting Stronger: Muscular Strength 2-Day Activity Log

   ➤ Reaching the Pyramid: Daily Nutrition Log

✔ **Goal-Setting Process—Study and Activity Guide**

✔ **Physical Fitness—Study and Activity Guide**

✔ **Fitness for Life—Study and Activity Guide**

✔ **Healthy Lifestyles—Study and Activity Guide**

✔ **Muscular Strength and Endurance—Study and Activity Guide**

Many students are interested in the reasons they should exercise regularly and plan a diet that follows national dietary guidelines. They also want to know what benefits can be derived from a well-designed exercise and nutrition program. The activities presented in Section 5 provide each student with multiple opportunities to monitor current exercise and dietary practices, along with gaining knowledge related to setting goals for the future. As students complete each personal log, work sheet, or task, they should be given an opportunity to review the information with teachers and discuss possible changes. (Each student will need five copies of the "Daily Nutrition Log," to record a week's nutrition—"Day 1," "Day 2," etc.) To facilitate this review, print and nonprint resources should be made available so students can research topics of interest and develop a resource file.

| Fitness Activities | Skill Development | Games That Teach | Healthy Lifestyles | Keeping Track |

ACTIVITY: LIFESTYLE TAG

Focus/ Knowledge Skill	Equipment Needed	Suggested Grade Levels
This lesson presents physical activities involving students in a review of risk-taking and healthy-lifestyle behaviors.	8 cone markers 8 jump ropes, dumbbells, volleyballs, basketballs, juggling equipment Activity Cards	Grades 4–8.

Success Notes Each day, students are confronted with various choices related to lifestyle behaviors. To increase student learning, introduce or review positive and negative effects of various activities, and compare and contrast the health-related risk factors and healthy physical activities.

MAKING IT WORK

Before students begin the activity, present basic information regarding health-risk behaviors related to smoking, use of alcohol and other drugs, and maintaining a high percentage of body fat. Ask students to list what they believe to be the effects or physical symptoms of these risk factors on their lifestyle and health. After reviewing risky behaviors, discuss positive health practices. Have students list what they believe to be the effects of physical activity and physical fitness on their lifestyle and health. Discuss, compare, and contrast the two lists.

To begin the physical activity portion of the lesson, post the activity cards (see reproducible masters) in various locations around the facility. Have students find a space within the boundary of a basketball court. Choose three to four students to be "it."

On the "go" signal, students begin to jog (you can also make use of other locomotor activities) randomly within the playing area. The "its," using the same locomotor activity, move about trying to tag others. The first time a person is tagged, he or she must stop, do 25 jumping jacks, then resume jogging. When tagged a second time, a student must immediately go to a station, read the card aloud, and do the activity, then reenter the game. When tagged for a second, third, or fourth time, students go directly to a station they have not previously gone to.

After approximately 2 minutes, change "its," and briefly review some of the risk and health factors.

Note: A foam frisbee can be held by the "its" to tag (not throw and hit) a person—thus eliminating personal touching.

Risk Factor 1

Smoking

1. Take 15 deep breaths.
2. Cough 20 times.

Risk Factor 2

Body Fat

1. Jog in place for 60 seconds.
2. Jog in place for 30 seconds, holding a 5-pound weight in each hand.

Risk Factor 3

Substance Abuse

1. Close one eye and try to throw a ball at a target 15 feet away.

2. Repeat alternating eye closures.

Healthy Behavior 1

Cardiovascular Fitness

Jump rope for two minutes.

Healthy Behavior 2

Muscular Strength

1. Do 60 seconds of push-ups.
2. Do 60 seconds of curl-ups.

Healthy Behavior 3

Flexibility

Do the "back-saver" sit and reach—hold 30 seconds each leg.

Healthy Behavior 4

Skill Challenge

Choose a physical activity you would like to participate in:

- Basketball "spot-shot" for 1 minute.
- Volleyball "wall-set" for 1 minute.
- Juggle scarves or cubes for 1 minute.

© 2000 by Parker Publishing Company

Healthy Behavior 5

Cardiovascular Fitness

Do the "ball-hop" between the end line and foul line for 1 minute.

| Fitness Activities | Skill Development | Games That Teach | Healthy Lifestyles | Keeping Track |

ACTIVITY: PERSONAL LOGS: KEEPING TRACK OF YOUR HEALTHY LIFESTYLE

Focus/ Knowledge Skill	Equipment Needed	Suggested Grade Levels
Keeping track of daily activities, lifestyle patterns, and habits; analysis of items recorded in relationship to positive health and fitness patterns	Specific "Personal Log" for each student	Grades 5–8. Modifications for grade levels: Modify for reading and activity levels as appropriate for your class.

Success Notes Students are very interested in keeping track of their personal habits; however, at this age, they are also very self-conscious. To keep participation and success at a maximum level, provide positive individual feedback. Allow students the opportunity to complete self-analysis of their activities and compare to what research says is best.

MAKING IT WORK

Your role in these activities is to explain, provide resources, give encouragement, and facilitate students during their participation in these projects. The following steps offer a successful format to follow.

1. Give students resources containing information on the importance of the activity to be focused on; for example, nutrition, physical activity, or other lifestyle behaviors.

2. Discuss the importance of the activity and how maintaining the log can be used as a baseline for setting goals.

3. Demonstrate how the log is to be kept and how you will work with the student to analyze the results.

4. When students have completed their logs, ask them to write down positive and negative items they discover.

5. After they have recorded information, ask students to analyze the data and write comments on ways to improve or to give themselves positive "self-messages" on their successes.

Recreational Activity Log

FOLLOW THE BASICS:

1. Do some kind of physical activity at least three or four days each week.

2. Keep track of your physical activity during this quarter, 8 weeks, and try to earn as many points as possible.

3. Remember, you cannot make up for a lack of activity one week with a large amount the next.

ABOUT THIS LOG:

1. Look at the table below and determine how many points you will earn for each activity.

2. To get credit for the activity points, you must be an active participant for the minimum time listed.

3. Record your points in the appropriate area.

4. If you reach the recommended maximum during a week, celebrate your success (5th and 6th grade, 15 points; 7th and 8th grade, 20 points).

5. Bring your "Log" to school each Monday so we can analyze your progress.

ACTIVITIES AND POINTS:

Activity	Minutes	Points	Activity	Minutes	Points
Basketball	25	2	Badminton	30	1
Cycling	15	2	Dancing	30	2
Aerobics	20	2	Gymnastics	30	2
Step Aerobics	15	2	Jogging	20	2
Rope Jumping	15	2	Roller Blading	20	1
Skating	20	1	Swimming—Laps	15	2
Tennis	20	2	Walking—Fast	20	2
Walking—Slow	20	1	Martial Arts	20	1
Weight Training	20	1	Volleyball	25	2
Skiing—X-Country	15	2	Skiing—Down Hill	25	1

Recreational Activity Log

For

_____

Name

Record your points and total. Did you make the goal?

	Mon	Tue	Wed	Thurs	Fri	Sat	Sun	Total
Week 1								
Week 2								
Week 3								
Week 4								
Week 5								
Week 6								
Week 7								
Week 8								

Total
Points

Being Flexible

For _____
Name

To increase your flexibility, you must use a daily program of specific flexibility exercises. Remember, warm-up exercises are not the same as exercises designed to increase flexibility. Keep track of your flexibility exercises for one week using this log. Use another "log" sheet for the second and third weeks.

Points to remember: • Slow stretching is best—hold the stretch position for 20–30 seconds; don't bounce.
• Stretch each joint in all directions in which the joint moves.
• Breathe while stretching—don't hold your breath.
• Increase the range of motion over a period of weeks.

Complete and have checked before beginning your program:

• Three exercises designed to increase flexibility in the shoulders and arms are:

_____

• Three exercises to increase flexibility in the back and abdomen are:

_____

• Three exercises to increase flexibility in the hips, upper leg (front and back), and lower leg are:

_____

Now you may begin to design and implement your flexibility program.

Good Luck!!!

217

Daily Flexibility Log

For

_____

Name

List up to three flexibility exercises, from your approved list, that you do each day

DAY	Upper Body			Back and Abdomen			Hips, and Legs		
Monday	1.			1.			1.		
	2.			2.			2.		
	3.			3.			3.		
Tuesday	1.			1.			1.		
	2.			2.			2.		
	3.			3.			3.		
Wednesday	1.			1.			1.		
	2.			2.			2.		
	3.			3.			3.		
Thursday	1.			1.			1.		
	2.			2.			2.		
	3.			3.			3.		
Friday	1.			1.			1.		
	2.			2.			2.		
	3.			3.			3.		
Saturday	1.			1.			1.		
	2.			2.			2.		
	3.			3.			3.		
Sunday	1.			1.			1.		
	2.			2.			2.		
	3.			3.			3.		

Activity Log

For

_____

Name

Keep a record of your physical activity habits for one week. Remember to complete the activity listed on the bottom of your log.

Day	List the physical activities and duration for each day.	Targeted Fitness Area	Future Changes
Monday			
Tuesday			
Wednesday			
Thursday			
Friday			
Saturday			

Write a one-page summary of your activities. Include what went well, why it went well, benefits to you.

How Did You Spend Your Time?

For

_____
Name

Record both physical and nonphysical activity and the amount of time you spent on each during each time period.

Time Period	Day 1 Act.	Day 1 Time	Day 2 Act.	Day 2 Time	Day 3 Act.	Day 3 Time	Day 4 Act.	Day 4 Time	Day 5 Act.	Day 5 Time
6 am–8 am										
8am–noon										
noon–3 pm										
3 pm–6 pm										
6 pm–10 pm										
10 pm–6 am										
Total time:	XXX		XXX		XXX		XXX		XXX	

Personal Goal Progress Log

For

_____
Name

It is important to keep track of the progress you are making towards achieving your goals. On this log, write down your accomplishments, any adjustments in your plan or goal, and your rewards. Remember, you a achieve a long-term goal by achieving short-term goals along the way.

Long-Term Goal: _____

Short-Term Goal: _____

****

Date	List Your Accomplishments and Progress	Rewards

Describe any adjustments to your plan or goal. _____

221

Weekly Aerobics Program

2 Points	
Walking	30 min
Cycling	20 min
Tennis	
Basketball	20 min
Soccer	
Rollerblading	20 min

3 Points	
Rope Skipping	20 min
Jogging	20 min
Swimming	20 min
Stair Climbing	20 min
Rowing	20 min

For _____

Name

Other continuous activities can count. Ask your teacher.

Day	Activity	Duration	Comments	Points
Monday				
Tuesday				
Wednesday				
Thursday				
Friday				
Saturday				
Sunday				

Goal: 15 points
per week

Totals: _____

Getting Stronger: Muscular Strength 2-Day Activity Log

Dates _____

For

Name _____

Day	Upper Body Strength			Abdominals and Back			Legs		
	Activity	Reps.	Sets	Activity	Reps.	Sets	Activity	Reps.	Sets
	Push-Up (2 types) (list type) ___ ___			Curl-Ups			1/2 Squats		
	Pull-Up (2 grips) (list type) ___ ___			Crunches			Lunges		
	Dips Bench or Chair			Cross-Over Crunch			Your Choice ___		
Day	Push-Up			Curl-Ups			1/2 Squats		
	Pull-Up			Crunches			Lunges		
	Dips			Cross-Over Crunch			Your Choice ___		

223

Reaching the Pyramid: Daily Nutrition Log

For _____
Name

Write down everything you eat or drink (except water) during the entire day. Check at the end of each day if you have "reached the pyramid" for that day. Keep this log for 5 days, and see how you have done. Are some days better than others? Why? Can you make changes? Answer those questions on a separate sheet after you have complete this log.

Day	Breakfast	Snack	Lunch	Snack	Dinner	Snack

Days Totals:

Breads (6–11 servings) _____ servings
Vegetables (3–5 servings) _____ servings

Fruits (2–4 servings) _____ servings
Dairy Products (2–3 servings) _____ servings
Meat, Poultry, Fish (2–3 servings) _____ servings

Groups in which you reached the recommendations: _____ _____ _____

Areas needing improvement: _____ _____

ACTIVITY: GOAL-SETTING PROCESS— STUDY AND ACTIVITY GUIDE

Focus/ Knowledge Skill	Equipment Needed	Suggested Grade Levels
To develop an understanding of the importance of setting personal and group goals, and the process involved	"Goal-Setting Study and Activity Guide" for each student Additional resource material regarding goal setting, as available	Grades 5–8. Modifications for grade levels: Students in grades 5 and 6 should set short-term rather than long-term goals.

Success Notes To emphasize the importance of setting personal and group goals, student must be given opportunities to utilize the process. During skill- and fitness-development activities and units, the goal-setting process should be used. Sample record sheets are provided in the "Fitness Activities" and Skill Development" sections.

MAKING IT WORK

The main focus of this study guide is to provide students with a basic understanding of the need to set goals and the process involved. To provide the knowledge base for student activities, the following class discussions should take place along with the individual or group work on the "Study Guide."

Discussion 1: What are goals? Goals serve as a guide and give each person or group something to work toward. They can help each person do her or his best. There are short-term and long-term goals.

Discussion 2: What is the goal-setting process? Goals are based on what a person or group wants and believes in, a realistic analysis of a starting point, and the realistic visualization of where the person or group wants to be. The process involves setting a pattern of short-term goals designed to reach the long-term goal. Each step along the way is evaluated and modified.

Students need a lot of assistance in the development of their initial goals. Most will have little experience with the process, therefore, when using the study guide, discussions and analysis of the process should take place after each activity.

SETTING GOALS—THE PROCESS

GOALS—WHAT ARE THEY AND WHY DO WE NEED THEM??

Almost anything you want to do now or in the future can be a personal goal. It might be passing a test, saving money to buy something special, getting into better physical shape, or making a team. Goals serve as a guide for what you want and give you a target to strive toward. Goals can be either short term or long term. They can be for you, individually, or for a group. No matter what type of goal you set, it will involve using the goal-setting process and taking personal responsibility for making proper decisions about your actions.

SHORT-TERM GOALS

Short-term goals are those that you set as a way either to achieve a long-term goal or to help achieve something in a short period of time. They may be reached in a few days or a few weeks. Short-term goals are usually very specific, like passing a math test next week or jogging 20 minutes three different times this week.

LONG-TERM GOALS

Long-term goals usually take a long time to achieve—maybe even years—and are achievable by meeting a series of short-term goals. Some examples of long-term goals might be to attend a specific university, get an A for a semester grade, or work out and eat properly to achieve a lower percent of body fat.

ACTIVITY

Choose one personal short-term goal and answer the following questions about it.

GOAL STATEMENT:_____

_____

_____

WHAT ARE YOUR TIME LINES TO MEET THIS GOAL? _____

_____

HOW WILL ACHIEVING THIS GOAL BE GOOD FOR YOU? _____

_____

_____

Setting goals is like walking up a series of stairs. When you reach the top floor, you have achieved your goal. If the top step is the achievement of a long-term goal, think of each lower step as a short-term goal. Take a look at the example below. Think about a long-term goal you might like to achieve and the steps or short-term goals that may be necessary.

EXAMPLE:

Long-Term Goal: Be able to jog 5 times per week for 30 minutes

Plan: Week one—jog 3 times for 15 minutes each.
Week two—jog 5 times for 15 minutes each.
Week three—jog 3 times for 20 minutes each.
Week four—jog 5 times for 20 minutes each.
Week five—jog 5 times for 25 minutes each.
Week six—jog 3 times for 30 minutes each.
Week seven—jog 5 times for 30 minutes each.

WEEK 7 ____

WEEK 6 ____

WEEK 5 ____

WEEK 4 ____

WEEK 3 ____

WEEK 2 ____

WEEK 1 ____

To begin establishing good personal goals, you must understand what you want and how to get it. To accomplish this you *must*:

1. **Examine your desire to improve:** This is the most important factor in the goal setting process. If you do not want to improve or to achieve a goal, it won't happen. Your parents, friends, and teachers cannot set or achieve the goals for you; they can only help you achieve what you want.

2. **Believe in yourself:** If you truly believe that you can do something—have the will power—you have a much better chance of achieving your goal. If you believe you cannot achieve something, you probably won't be able to do it.

3. **Know where you are when you start:** Knowing your starting point is very important in setting either short- or long-term goals. For example, if you want to increase your muscular strength, you have to have some idea of how much strength you currently have.

4. **Set realistic and achievable goals:** It is important for your goals to be realistic and achievable. If you set a goal that is too hard to reach, you may become

discouraged and give up trying. On the other hand, if your goal is too easy to reach, you can lose interest in setting goals. Remember, a realistic goal is one that is both reachable and challenging.

5. **Write down your goals in detail, and list the benefits of achieving them:** Writing your goals down will help you in making specific plans to achieve them. You should also put your goals in a place where you can easily see them several times each day. Writing down the benefits you will gain from achieving the goal will also help you work hard to accomplish them. It will make your desire stronger, which, in turn, will make your belief in yourself even stronger. An example would be:

   GOAL: To improve my cardiovascular endurance so I can jog two miles without stopping.

   BENEFITS: Increase my self-esteem

   Have a healthier heart and lungs

   Improve my body image

   Increase my total energy

   Be able to keep up with my friends

6. **Make a daily plan:** Write down what you are going to do each day to move closer to achieving your goal, what can keep you from achievement, and how to overcome the obstacles.

7. **Evaluate your progress and your goals:** Take time to check on how you are progressing toward your goal. If you find you have set your goal too high, change the goal or modify how you are going to achieve it. Remember, an important part of the goal-setting process is to establish realistic goals. If you find that a goal, short- or long-term, is not realistic for you, change it. Adding a few more steps to the progression may help you achieve the final goal.

ACTIVITY

Look back to the short-term goal you established and answer the following questions.

WHAT ARE THE BENEFITS OF REACHING MY GOAL? _____

_____

_____

_____

WHERE AM I NOW—BASELINE INFORMATION? _____

_____

_____

_____

WHAT STEPS SHOULD I TAKE TO ACHIEVE MY GOAL? _____

_____

_____

_____

WHAT THINGS MIGHT GET IN MY WAY, AND HOW CAN I OVERCOME THEM?

_____

_____

_____

WHAT ARE MY TIME LINES?   Beginning date: _____

Accomplishment date:_____

Review dates (between beginning and accomplishment dates) _____

_____

_____

_____

HOW WILL I POSITIVELY REWARD MYSELF FOR ACHIEVING MY GOALS?

_____

_____

_____

ACTIVITY: PHYSICAL FITNESS— STUDY AND ACTIVITY GUIDE

Focus/ Knowledge Skill	Equipment Needed	Suggested Grade Levels
The understanding of personal fitness in relationship to the development of a healthy lifestyle: target heart rate, goal setting, activity selection	"Study and Activity Guide" for each student Support material as available at school or through technology available to all students	Grades 7–8

Success Notes Although all students in class will have the same Study Guide, individuals should develop their own programs to meet personal goals and needs. If students do not want to share their program or goals with others, they should not be required to do so. As the use of study guides involves reading and the ability to comprehend, the use of partners or study groups should be considered where some students have not achieved a reading level to fully understand the material presented

MAKING IT WORK

The Physical Fitness Study Guide is designed to provide a basic understanding of how physical fitness affects one's life. It should be used in conjunction with basic fitness activities, discussions of nutrition, and the development of healthy lifestyle goals.

After providing a basic overview of the meaning and importance of physical fitness, ask students to read each section and do the activities. After completing the activities, discuss the responses to the activities and check for understanding through questioning. Do not have students complete the final activity at this time.

During the activity portion of the class, have students use the information presented in the study guide; for example, determining target heart rate, monitoring heart rate during exercise, choosing appropriate exercises.

After students have had approximately one week of experience in using the information and discussing the need to set goals and plan for daily activity, have them complete the final activity. Rather than discussing this activity, tell students that this is their personal plan. They can put it on the wall in their room, on the refrigerator, or in a place where they can refer to it each day.

PHYSICAL FITNESS—THE BASICS

Think of your body as a car. To keep it running in top condition, you must put the proper fuel in it, keep the outside washed and waxed, and keep the engine running smoothly with necessary maintenance. If you don't do these things, you will eventually have to replace the car. Your body requires the same type of care. You must eat the proper type and amount of food—your body's fuel, keep it clean, and exercise on a regular basis to keep it running smoothly. Since you can't replace your body like a car, it is best to keep it tuned by eating a proper diet, exercising, and getting enough rest.

Exercise helps maintain your body by strengthening the muscles—including your heart, burning off excess calories, improving your flexibility, and increasing your self-esteem. An effective exercise program must become a part of your regular schedule if you are going to be at your best. It also must be fun and done at an appropriate level so you don't get too tired or sore.

ACTIVITY:

Write a short phrase that best describes your current level of fitness.

_____

_____

_____

_____

_____

In one or two sentences, describe what exercise means to you. _____

_____

_____

_____

_____

One of the most important things for you to understand about yourself is that you were born with a specific body type that you cannot change. Some people are naturally thin, stocky, wide in the hip, tall, or short. You can't change the size of your bones or your height, can you? But you can shape your body by working on things you can improve, such as your muscular strength, cardiovascular endurance, flexibility, and amount of body fat.

Before you begin an exercise program, you should do several things.

1. Check with your doctor. This will help you find out if you have any medical problems that need to be taken into consideration when planning your exercise program.

231

2. Set reasonable goals and start slowly. Start doing something that you know you will do. Remember, don't start with too much or you will "burn out" quickly. Set a short-term goal that you can achieve within a week or two. After achieving this goal, set another.

3. Treat yourself with respect. Exercise when it is comfortable and convenient for you. Make your exercise time fun by asking a friend to do it with you. Also, give yourself a reward for good effort.

4. Do what you like. If you do activities that you enjoy, your chances of sticking to an exercise program, and making it a regular part of your life, are much greater.

A good exercise program includes an appropriate warm-up time, stretching, cardiovascular exercises, muscular strength activities, and a good cool-down period. An average program should last about 45 to 60 minutes. Remember, at least 10 minutes should be used for warm-up and cool-down.

When planning your program, take into consideration three recommendations to get the most out of your exercising:

1. Frequency—three to five days every week

2. Duration—20 to 30 minutes of continuous aerobic activity depending on the intensity

3. Intensity—60 to 80 percent of your maximum heart rate for cardiovascular endurance activities

ACTIVITY

What is you favorite way to get exercise? _____

_____

_____

Why is this your favorite way? _____

_____

_____

_____

Does it include parts of a good exercise program? Which ones? _____

_____

_____

_____

_____

What, if anything, is missing?_____

_____

_____

_____

_____

Cardiovascular endurance is developed though aerobic exercises. These exercises get you to use your entire body. They strengthen your heart and lungs by making you breathe deeply and your heart beat faster. When you are exercising aerobically, your blood vessels expand, carrying more oxygen to the working muscles so they can keep working.

It is important, when developing the cardiovascular endurance part of your program, that you know your target heart rate. This is the number of times your heart should beat in one minute to get the maximum benefit. Remember duration and frequency also.

ACTIVITY

Calculate your target heart rate—THR.

	Boys	**Girls**
	220	205
subtract 1/2 your age	−	−
	_____	_____

This is your maximum heart rate.

Multiply by:	× .70	× .70
	_____	_____

Your Target Heart Rate

ACTIVITY

A cardiovascular activity I can do is. . . _____

_____.

Another great cardiovascular activity would be _____

_____.

Muscular strength and endurance are other components of physical fitness. Muscular strength is your muscles' ability to apply force, and muscular endurance is the muscles' ability to apply force for a period of time.

ACTIVITY

A muscular strength and endurance activity I can do is _____

_____.

Being fit means many things, including:

1. Your muscles have better tone, strength, and endurance.
2. Your posture and overall appearance are improved.
3. Your digestive system improves, and your appetite is controlled.
4. Your joints are more flexible and allow greater ease and range of movement.
5. Your sleep is sounder.
6. Your self-image and self-esteem are improved.

ACTIVITY

1. A physical fitness change I would like to make is _____

_____.

2. By making this change, I will get _____

_____.

3. The things, people or situations that might get in my way are _____

_____.

4. What can I do to change these things? _____

_____.

5. To make this change possible, I will _____

_____

_____.

6. The people who can help me are _____

_____

_____.

7. I will reward myself for progress toward being more healthy by _____

_____

_____

_____.

| Fitness Activities | Skill Development | Games That Teach | Healthy Lifestyles | Keeping Track |

ACTIVITY: FITNESS FOR LIFE— STUDY AND ACTIVITY GUIDE

Focus/ Knowledge Skill	Equipment Needed	Suggested Grade Levels
The importance of actively participating in physical activities on a daily basis is emphasized. This lesson is designed to assist students in becoming more aware of activities they can do to promote physical well-being throughout their lives.	Overhead projector and screen. Student work sheets and resource material.	Grades 7–8 Modifications for grade levels: Grade 7 students may focus on the physical components; grade 8 students focus on emotional and social components.

Success Notes Students must see the relationship of physical activity and health to their current lifestyle and well being. As they are asked to analyze activity patterns, focus on activities currently participated in and how they relate to the future.

MAKING IT WORK

Begin the class discussion by defining "lifetime activities" and one or two benefits derived from active participation. Give students a few minutes to generate two or three additional benefits from participation in physical activities, and to write them down on their "Fitness for Life" work sheets. Discuss benefits, and have the students complete their work sheets by listing activities they think would fit the definition of "lifetime activities." Students will generally list only sport-related activities. Use the teacher information to generate discussions related to activities other than sports that require physical activity. Ask students to work in groups to generate ten to fifteen activities they do outside of school that meet the definition of "lifetime activities."

As a homework assignment, have students speak with family and other adults to determine what physical activities they participate in. During the next class period, discuss the outcome of their survey. Also, discuss why they think most people participate in individual activities as they get older, rather than keeping with the more traditional team activities. At the conclusion of the discussion, have students complete their "Activity Analysis" sheets, and follow up with a discussion of activities listed and the various benefits.

FITNESS FOR LIFE
(TEACHER INFORMATION)

Definition: Activities an individual can participate in at almost any age that do not require a group. At most, these activities usually involve one, two, or three people. Examples include walking, tennis, bowling, and jogging.

Benefits:

Physical: Help to gain, maintain, or improve:

- *Muscular strength*: the ability of a muscle to overcome a resistance (lifting a heavy object)
- *Muscular endurance*: the ability of a muscle to overcome a resistance over time (repeated lifting of a heavy object)
- *Flexibility*: the ability of an individual to move joints in a range of motion
- *Cardiovascular (anaerobic)*: the ability of an individual to perform a high-intensity activity for a short period of time (sprinting)
- *Cardiovascular (aerobic)*: the ability to perform moderate to low-intensity activities for a longer period of time—15 minutes to an hour or longer
- *Coordination and balance*: the ability to perform various complex movements at once
- *Blood pressure*
- *Resting heart rate and heart rate response*
- *Physiological functions* (digestion, respiration, and circulation)

Emotional: help to gain, maintain, or improve:

- Management of stress
- Management of conflicts or problems
- Self-esteem
- Self-discipline

Social: Help to gain, maintain, or improve:

- Social relationships—developing new friendships
- Feeling comfortable when alone
- Enhanced communication

Why people participate in individual activities as they get older

- Not as easy to get a group together because of work schedules
- Physical and physiological functions of the body change—less ability to participate in more vigorous activities
- Greater variety and availability of activities, such as swimming, hiking, and skiing
- More family, community, and personal commitments

236

FITNESS FOR LIFE

I. **Definition** – Activities an individual can participate in at almost any age that do not require a group for success. These activities usually involve one, two, or three people at the most. Examples include tennis, bowling, and gardening.

II. **Benefits**

Physical: Help to gain, maintain, or improve:

_____

_____

_____

_____

Social: Help to gain, maintain, or improve:

_____

_____

_____

_____

Emotional: Help to gain, maintain, or improve:

_____

_____

_____

_____

III. **Lifetime Activities**

_____

_____

_____

_____

Name:_____

ACTIVITY ANALYSIS

Take three activities (at least one that is not sports related) and write what you believe are the benefits from participation. Be certain to include physical, social, and emotional benefits. Use the information from your "Fitness for Life" Work Sheet to help you with the analysis. Use additional paper if necessary.

Example: **Gardening**

Physical	Social	Emotional
Flexibility—bending	Member of a club	Handling stress
Coordination/balance		Self-discipline
Muscular endurance		Feeling comfortable when alone

Activity 1: _____

Physical	Social	Emotional

Activity 2: _____

Physical	Social	Emotional

Activity 3: _____

Physical	Social	Emotional

ACTIVITY: HEALTHY LIFESTYLES— STUDY AND ACTIVITY GUIDE

Focus/ Knowledge Skill	Equipment Needed	Suggested Grade Levels
This activity provides each student with an overview of basic lifestyle choices and concepts that are part of developing a healthy lifestyle.	"Study and Activity Guide" for each student	Grades 6–7 Modifications for grade levels: Make sure that all students understand the vocabulary presented.

Success Notes Have students discuss their ideas for the general development of a healthy lifestyle. Remember that students should not be required to discuss specifics of their lifestyle unless they want to. The use of study groups or partners can assist students with reading and comprehension difficulties.

MAKING IT WORK

To be able to live a healthy lifestyle, students must first understand what personal wellness is, and its importance to their lives. This activity will help students analyze their habits and current lifestyle in relationship to basic health facts. **Note:** Students may volunteer information for this activity, but they should be told that they are not required to share it.

To ensure that all students have a basic understanding of the concepts to be used in the analysis of their lifestyle, the first class activity should consist of brainstorming for the basic health factors leading to a healthy lifestyle. Have students write down their ideas on the first page of the study guide, then list these concepts on the board and allow time for discussion after all ideas have been listed. The next step is to present the list of health factors provided on the study guide. Ask the class to compare and contrast the two lists.

After completing the first two steps, ask students to read the study guide and do the other activities listed. After the activities have been completed, provide time for class discussion and interaction related to the activity topics.

Enhancement:

Some students may be ready to begin setting short-terms goals. These students should be given information on the goal-setting process and allowed to go ahead.

HEALTHY LIFESTYLES— OFF TO A GREAT START

To live a healthy lifestyle, you must first understand what personal wellness is. What do you think it is?

ACTIVITY

What do you think personal wellness is?

_____

_____

_____

These are a few definitions of personal wellness that other students have decided upon.

1. Personal wellness is the ability to focus in on your current lifestyle and learn how to make changes that will benefit you and allow you to be all that you can and want to be.

2. Personal wellness takes all areas in one's life and gives them meaning.

3. Personal wellness encompasses the whole body—mental, physical, emotional, and spiritual.

4. Personal wellness gives you the freedom to be who you want to be.

Who, of all the people you know, doesn't want to live a long, healthy, and happy life? No one, right? Developing and maintaining a healthy lifestyle means being concerned with all the various aspects of your health. (Look back at the "healthy lifestyles" activities you have already completed.)

ACTIVITY

List several things you believe could help develop a healthy lifestyle.

_____

_____

_____

Some basic health factors that can lead to the development of a healthy lifestyle are:
1. Getting regular exercise at an appropriate level
2. Eating a well-balanced diet
3. Getting enough sleep each night—8 hours
4. Maintaining a healthy weight for your height and build

5. Not smoking or using alcohol or other drugs

6. Having regular check-ups with your doctor and dentist

7. Acting safely and reducing risks

8. Communicating and cooperating appropriately with others

9. Being involved in activities that you find rewarding

10. Managing stress in a positive manner

ACTIVITY

Did you list any of these items on your list? Which ones?

_____

_____

_____

Which ones do you do now?

_____

_____

Which ones could you do if you had some help?

_____

_____

Whom can you ask for help in changing your lifestyle?

_____

_____

ACTIVITY

Write your definition of a healthy lifestyle.

_____

_____

_____

_____

_____

ACTIVITY: MUSCULAR STRENGTH AND ENDURANCE—STUDY AND ACTIVITY GUIDE

Focus/ Knowledge Skill	Equipment Needed	Suggested Grade Levels
The concepts involved in developing muscular strength and endurance with practical applications: differentiate types of strength conditioning; learn how to enhance activity participation	"Study and Activity Guide" for each student	Grades 6–8 Modifications for grade levels: Students may benefit from working with study partners or in small groups.

Success Notes Provide enough print and nonprint resources for students to follow-up. Check with students, and ask how the knowledge gained from this packet can be used to enhance their individual performance.

MAKING IT WORK

Begin this activity by having a brief discussion on how the muscles of the body work:

- Which muscles are the strongest? Why?
- Which muscles are used the most? Used the least?
- Are all muscles alike? (heart, biceps, triceps, hamstrings, etc.)

Provide students with definitions of:

Muscular Strength: The amount of force a muscle or muscle group can exert in one maximum effort.

Muscular Endurance: The amount of force a muscle or muscle group can exert over a period of time

Ask students to read each section of the packet carefully before doing the activities. If they have any questions, make time each day to give answers. It is also helpful to provide a bibliography of resources located in the school library or accessible via local technology.

EXERCISES THAT BUILD MUSCULAR STRENGTH AND ENDURANCE

Be sure to read each section carefully before doing the activities.

To increase the strength and endurance of your muscles, you have to work them harder (intensity), longer (duration), and on a schedule (regularity). You also must exercise muscles individually, or in groups, with exercises specifically designed for those muscles (specificity). This means that, if you are using weights, you could increase the number of repetitions and/or the amount of weight used while working a specific muscle or muscle group.

There are three major types of exercises designed to increase muscular strength and endurance. They are:

1. *Isotonic Exercises*: These exercises cause the muscle to lengthen or shorten through movement. You can see the muscle move when exercising—lifting a weight.

2. *Isometric Exercises*: These exercises lengthen or shorten the muscle without movement. You usually cannot see the muscle working—pushing hard against a wall.

3. *Isokinetic Exercises*: The muscle contracts through a full range of motion, with equal resistance through the entire range—performing a bench press with weights.

WHY BUILD MUSCULAR STRENGTH?

❏ To replace fat with muscle

❏ To help shape and tone your body

❏ To help you perform physical activities at a higher level

❏ To help increase your feeling of self-worth

WHAT EXERCISES HELP BUILD MUSCULAR STRENGTH?

• Performing a small number of repetitions with maximum resistance

• Using the concept of specificity—using only a limited number of muscles at one time.

• Increasing the resistance/weight after you can perform a small number of repetitions easily.

WHAT EXERCISES HELP BUILD MUSCULAR ENDURANCE?

• Performing a large number of repetitions with light resistance

• Increasing weight when appropriate but keeping the number of repetitions high

• Using the concept of specificity along with general exercises

ACTIVITY

Give the definition and an example of each of the following types of strength training.

Isotonic Exercises: _____

_____

_____

_____

Isometric Exercises: _____

_____

_____

_____

Isokinetic Exercise: _____

_____

_____

_____

Can you list an advantage to each type of exercise?

Isotonic Exercises: _____

Isometric Exercises: _____

Isokinetic Exercises: _____

ACTIVITY

Next to each activity write the number of one or more of the three major muscle groups—or a combination of all—that are used **most often.**

MAJOR MUSCLE GROUPS ARE:

1. Upper Body: arms, chest, back, neck
2. Lower Body: legs
3. Abdominal: stomach muscles
4. Combination of muscle groups

_____ baseball		_____ cycling
_____ football		_____ soccer
_____ tennis		_____ wrestling
_____ swimming		_____ skating
_____ skiing		_____ volleyball
_____ jogging		_____ golf
_____ juggling		_____ orienteering

ACTIVITY

Choose three physical activities that you participate in or would like to participate in. What exercises would you do to improve your muscular strength and endurance for each activity?

Activity   **Exercises**

* *

1. _____

   _____

2. _____

   _____

3. _____

   _____

SECTION 6

Keeping Track

MEANINGFUL ASSESSMENT

- **Offer** assessments that are interactive and provide useful feedback to students.

- **Promote** accountability for being active and enhancing knowledge and skill.

- **Focus** on individual improvement.

KEEPING TRACK

✔ **Fit Quiz: Quizzes for Fitness-Related Concepts and Activities**
  ➤ Fit For Knowledge
  ➤ How's Your Aerobic IQ?
  ➤ Aerobic Endurance and You
  ➤ Muscular Strength and You
  ➤ Testing Your Strength
  ➤ Are You Flexible
  ➤ Know Your Composition
  ➤ How Can I Plan
  ➤ What Do Exercises and Activities Do For You
  ➤ Answer Key

✔ **Skill and Fitness Journals**
  ➤ Floor Hockey
  ➤ Soccer
  ➤ Basketball
  ➤ Softball
  ➤ Racket Sports
  ➤ Volleyball

✔ **Opinion Poll: Quizzes for Various Activities**
  ➤ Fitness
  ➤ Soccer
  ➤ Volleyball
  ➤ Badminton
  ➤ Pickleball
  ➤ Softball   ➤ Golf   ➤ Answer Key

Assessment in physical education should represent progress individual students have made toward achieving the objectives of class activities and meeting personal goals—not items or areas over which the student has little or no control and that do not accurately reflect stated class objectives. Although current practice finds numerous innovative assessment methods (peer video review, continual self-monitoring, or written progress journals), the items in Section 6 provide a more standardized approach. However, when using this approach, the successful teacher will combine these written tasks with other forms of activity-related assessments.

Fitness Activities	Skill Development	Games That Teach	Healthy Lifestyles	Keeping Track

ACTIVITY: FIT QUIZ: QUIZZES FOR FITNESS-RELATED CONCEPTS AND ACTIVITIES

Focus/ Knowledge Skill	Equipment Needed	Suggested Grade Levels
Students apply their knowledge of fitness by answering and discussing challenging questions: —general fitness —aerobic endurance —muscular strength —flexibility —body composition	"Fit Quiz" sheet for each student. "Fit Quiz" answer key	Grades 5–8 Modifications for grade levels: Students in grade 5 benefit from working in cooperative groups; older students can work individually or with partners.

Success Notes Before students complete a "Fit Quiz" activity, they should actively take part in activities related to the fitness component and be given direct instruction on the topic. See activities in Section 5, "Healthy Lifestyle."

MAKING IT WORK

Using the "Fit Quiz" is an excellent way to check student knowledge and generate active discussions related to the components of physical fitness and the development of a healthy lifestyle. To effectively use it for both learning and basic assessment, try following these steps.

1. Have students participate in activities designed to enhance the targeted fitness component.

2. During the introduction of the activity, discuss the concepts, muscles used, and benefits of participation and the development of a higher level of fitness.

3. Have students participate in a related activity from Section 5.

4. Provide time for group discussion related to the targeted fitness component.

5. Have students answer the "Fit Quiz" questions, individually or in groups.

6. Discuss student answers in relation to those mentioned on the "Answer Key." Students might have correct answers that differ from those on the key.

7. List answers on a poster board which can be posted on the wall and referred to during other activities related to this and other fitness components.

Fit Quiz

Name: _____

Fit For Knowledge

1. What muscle does a
"couch potato" sit on?

_____

2. What is the number-one
cause of premature death
in America?

_____

_____

3. What are the four components of health-related physical fitness?

_____

4. What are the specific names
of the muscles in your upper arm?

_____ (top side)

_____ (bottom side)

5. What activity that children do
most is closely associated
with obesity? _____

6. Put an X by the aerobic activities.

__weight lifting __circuit training

__walking __hiking

__swimming __jogging

__sprints __curl-ups

__golf __football

7. At what two times in a person's life do
cells multiply at their fastest rate?
_____ and _____

250

Fit Quiz

How's Your Aerobic IQ?

1. When you exercise, your heart and lungs' biggest job is to: _____

2. When your aerobic endurance is increased your heart:

○ pumps more blood
○ beats less often
○ is stronger
○ is healthier

3. Name two jobs of the lungs.

_____
_____

4. List three ways to improve your aerobic endurance

_____
_____
_____

5. Which of the following is the best aerobic conditioning activity?

○ fast, short sprints
○ playing football
○ long, slow jogs
○ tumbling

6. List two places on your body where you can measure your pulse rate.

_____
_____

7. Which athlete will probably build the most aerobic endurance?

○ soccer goalie
○ football lineman
○ baseball/softball field
○ distance swimmer

251

Fit Quiz

Name: _____

Aerobic Endurance and You

1. Name one important function of the heart, lungs, and blood vessels during exercise.

_____

2. List four aerobic endurance activities that you could do.

_____

_____

_____

_____

3. The exercise principle of overload when applied to aerobic endurance means:

_____

4. Give an example of progression in building an aerobic conditioning program.

_____

6. The term "target heart rate" means:

_____

7. Progression means to:

  ○ start easy and go for a long period
  ○ change from running to swimming
  ○ exercise harder or longer each week
  ○ play sports and exercise

5. To find your heart rate when counting your pulse for 6 seconds should you:

  ○ multiply by 2

  ○ add a zero

  ○ multiply by 10

  ○ double it

8. The general recommendation for level of effort to improve aerobic endurance is:

  60% to _____% of maximum pulse rate
  20 to _____ minutes of continuous exercise

© 2000 by Parker Publishing Company

Fit Quiz

Name: _____

MUSCULAR STRENGTH AND YOU

1. Specificity to improve muscular strength means:

_____

2. Exercising on a regular schedule to improve physical fitness is called

_____

3. Check three activities that can help build muscular strength.

- ○ curl-ups
- ○ shooting baskets
- ○ rope climbing
- ○ lifting weights
- ○ playing volleyball

4. Muscles are fastened to other parts of the body by:

_____

5. Muscular strength means:

_____

6. Which is the main job of muscles?

- ○ help you look good
- ○ move your bones
- ○ help to relax
- ○ keep you fit

7. Doing more or harder exercises over a period of weeks and months is:

_____

8. Working your muscles harder by lifting more or doing more repetitions is called:

_____

253

TESTING YOUR STRENGTH

1. What is the physical fitness principle of exercising hard enough to get a training effect called?

_____

2. What should you do before participating in a vigorous game or fitness activity?

_____

3. List four exercises that can help build arm and shoulder strength.

_____
_____
_____
_____

4. How many times per week should you exercise to build muscular strength?

_____

5. Check the statement that relates to muscular endurance.

○ the ability to move heavy weight once
○ the ability to play sports
○ the ability to lift weights
○ the ability to move something many times

6. What are the sections of a muscle called?

_____

7. Muscles usually contract:

○ by themselves
○ when they are cold
○ on a signal from the brain
○ when they are warmed up

Fit Quiz

Name: _____

ARE YOU FLEXIBLE?

1. List two body structures that help hold joints together and that need to be stretched.

_____

_____

2. Stretching before exercising will help:

○ build strength
○ avoid injuries
○ burn a lot of calories
○ build endurance

3. Joints and muscles are prepared for physical activity by: warming up and

_____

4. How often should you stretch?

_____

5. The best, and safest, way to stretch is:

○ slowly
○ holding the stretch position for 20–30 seconds
○ before and after exercise
○ quickly

6. Regular stretching permits you to perform better and improves the:

_____

7. Ligaments help hold _____ together while tendons anchor muscles to _____.

255

Fit Quiz

KNOW YOUR COMPOSITION

1. Extra fat on your body may be the result of:

○ eating too much
○ exercising too much
○ exercising too little
○ playing too many games

2. Energy is measured in:

_____

3. List four essential nutrients that should be included in your daily diet.

_____   _____

_____   _____

4. In most people, the amount of body fat can be controlled by:

_____

_____

5. Your body composition is determined by measuring both:

_____ mass

and

_____ mass

6. To reduce your saturated fat consumption, you should reduce the amount of foods eaten that are high in fat, such as:

_____

_____

_____

_____

© 2000 by Parker Publishing Company

Fit Quiz

Name: _____

HOW CAN IN PLAN?

If I jog 4 times each week for 30 minutes (about 3 miles) at 60% of my target heart rate and want to . . .

Complete the statement above by answering these questions.

* *

1. . . . increase my endurance (the ability to go longer), I should _____

   _____

   _____

2. . . . finish my workout in a shorter amount of time and get the same benefits, I should _____

   _____

   _____

3. . . . increase the intensity of my workout by raising my heart rate, I should_____

   _____

4. . . . begin working out again after an injury, I should _____

   _____

   _____

Fit Quiz

WHAT DO EXERCISES AND ACTIVITIES DO FOR YOU?

Listed below are some exercises and activities that you do in and outside of school. Think about each activity and how it helps you become healthier. Place an X in the column(s) that you believe best fits the activity.

ACTIVITY	Aerobic Endurance	Muscular Strength	Flexibility
Step Aerobics	_____	_____	_____
Low-Impact Aerobics	_____	_____	_____
Weight Training	_____	_____	_____
Basketball	_____	_____	_____
Soccer	_____	_____	_____
Jogging	_____	_____	_____
Rope Skipping	_____	_____	_____
Push-Ups	_____	_____	_____
Sit and Reach	_____	_____	_____
Orienteering	_____	_____	_____
Cycling	_____	_____	_____
Swimming	_____	_____	_____
Climbing	_____	_____	_____
Pickleball	_____	_____	_____

Answer Key

Fit for Knowledge

1. gluteus maximus
2. heart disease
3. muscular strength, aerobic endurance, flexibility, body composition
4. biceps (top), triceps (bottom)
5. watching tv or video games
6. walking, swimming, jogging, hiking, circuit training
7. birth, adolescence

How's Your Aerobic IQ?

1. get more oxygen to muscles
2. all
3. supply oxygen to muscles take in oxygen
4. jogging, walking, swimming, cycling, rope skipping, bench stepping, roller blading
5. long, slow jogs
6. wrist, side of neck, chest
7. distance swimmer

Aerobic Endurance and You

1. get oxygen to muscles
2. jogging, cycling, walking, swimming
3. raise pulse rate to target zone and keep it there long enough to get a training effect
4. going faster, longer, farther, and more often
5. add a zero
6. getting your heart rate to 60%–80% of maximum and keeping it there
7. start easy and go for long period, exercise harder or longer each week
8. 80%, 30 minutes

Muscular Strength and You

1. exercising a specific muscle
2. regularity
3. curl-ups, rope climbing, and lifting weights
4. tendons
5. moving a heavy weight once
6. move your bones
7. progression
8. progression

Answer Key

Testing Your Strength

1. overload
2. warm up
3. push-ups, pull-ups, rope climbing, specific weight training
4. three to five
5. the ability to move something many times
6. fibers
7. on a signal from the brain

Are You Flexible

1. ligaments, muscles
2. avoid injuries
3. stretching
4. daily
5. slowly, holding the stretch for 20–30 seconds before and after exercise
6. range of motion
7. joints, bones

Know Your Composition

1. eating too much, exercising too little
2. calories
3. proteins, vitamins, carbohydrates, minerals
4. eating less exercising more
5. fat
   lean
6. whole milk, fried foods, red meat

How Can I Plan?

1. jog for a longer amount of time.
2. increase the intensity of the workout.
3. jog faster or on a harder course.
4. go slowly and reduce the intensity and duration.

ACTIVITY: OPINION POLL: QUIZZES FOR VARIOUS ACTIVITIES

Focus/ Knowledge Skill	Equipment Needed	Suggested Grade Levels
Students apply their knowledge of sports skills, rules, and strategies. Students answer challenging questions that can lead to class discussions and further research projects.	"Opinion Poll" sheets for each student Pencils for each student	Grades 6–8 Modifications for grade levels: Students may benefit from working in cooperative groups.

Success Notes Before students answer an "Opinion Poll," provide them with a study guide containing the appropriate written information, classroom discussion, and opportunities to participate in each activity so that students understand the specific information and general concepts. Add questions that are fun, and specific to the class; for example, "What is the date of our fitness test?" "What is the name of the school mascot, and why was it chosen?"

MAKING IT WORK

The "Opinion Poll" is an excellent way to check for student understanding and generate discussions related to specific topics and activities. This form of assessment should be used not only to gather information on student progress, but, also to assist in planning for future programs. The following steps will help in using this assessment format effectively.

1. Provide each student with a study guide consisting of written information on the topic.
2. Review and discuss information contained in the study guide.
3. Have students participate in activities, making use of the information presented.
4. At the end of each activity session, discuss how they used the information in the study guide to participate successfully.
5. Have students answer the questions in the "Opinion Poll."
6. Discuss students' answers. Ask students if they see any carry-over from one activity to another.
7. Make use of the "Opinion Poll" for grading purposes.

Opinion Poll

Name _____

FITNESS

Complete these statements.

1. Aerobic exercise should be sustained for a minimum of _____ minutes ___ to ___ days per week to gain benefits.

2. The "target heart rate" represents _____% to _____% of a person's maximum heart rate.

3. The term aerobic means _____.

4. Anaerobic exercise is an activity that places short, intense demands for energy on our muscles. This type of exercise does not need _____ because it uses stored _____.

5. To increase muscle strength and bulk one would lift _____ weights with a _____ repetitions.

6. To improve muscle tone endurance one should lift _____ weights with _____ repetitions.

7. Duration means_____.

   Frequency means_____.

   Intensity means _____.

Why are duration, frequency, and intensity important considerations in developing your personal fitness program?

_____

_____

_____

Opinion Poll

Name _____

SOCCER

Complete these statements.

1. A regulation soccer team consists of _____ players.

2. Name four different parts of the body that a player may stop, control, pass, move the ball with. _____, _____, _____, _____

3. Describe the kick-off that begins a game.

   _____

   _____

   _____

   _____

4. A direct free kick is awarded for _____, _____, _____.

5. An indirect free kick is awarded for _____, _____, _____.

6. All players must be _____ yards away from the spot a penalty kick is taken from.

7. A goal may not be scored from an indirect kick until _____ _____.

Opinion Poll

Name _____

VOLLEYBALL

Complete these statements.

1. The object of volleyball is to send the ball over the net so the opposing team is unable to return it or _____.

2. Any part of the body _____ may be used to hit the ball.

3. A serve is made from the _____ of the court.

4. Each team may touch the ball _____ times before sending it over the net.

5. Describe what happens if a player:

   a. touches the net?_____

   b. touches the ball two consecutive times? _____

   c. crosses the center line when the ball is in play? _____

   d. "spikes" the ball above the opponents' court (reaches over the net)? _____

6. A game is played to _____ points.

7. If the score is tied at 14 to 14, describe what happens. _____
_____.

8. If two players on the same team touch the ball at the same time, it counts as _____.

Opinion Poll

Name _____

BADMINTON

Complete these statements.

1. Only the _____ can score a point.

2. To win a game, _____ points are needed.

3. On the serve, the shuttle (bird) must be hit _____ the waist.

4. A serve from the "right" service court must go into the _____ receiving court.

5. The server commits a fault when the _____ _____.

6. The receiver who commits a fault, _____.

7. List three types of "general" faults. _____, _____, _____.

8. In singles, the service court is always decided by the _____ score.

    a. If the score is an even number, the service is from the _____ court.

    b. If the score is an odd number, the service is from the _____ court.

Opinion Poll

Name _____

PICKLEBALL

Complete these statements.

1. Players must keep _____ behind the _____ line when serving.

2. The serve must be made _____ and the paddle must pass _____ the waist.

3. The server must hit the ball in the _____ on the serve; it is not allowed to _____ before hitting it.

4. All volleying must be done with players feet _____ the nonvolley zone.

5. The service is made _____ across court and must clear the _____.

6. The game is played to _____ points; a team must win by _____ points.

7. The receiving team must let the serve _____, and the receiving team must let the return of the serve _____.

8. List three faults: _____,

_____,

_____

© 2000 by Parker Publishing Company

Opinion Poll

Name _____

SOFTBALL

Complete these statements.

1. A softball field is _____ in size than a baseball field.

2. The infield positions are: _____, _____, _____, _____, _____, _____.

3. The outfield positions are: _____, _____, _____, _____. (in slow-pitch)

4. There are _____ players on a team.

5. Three ways of putting a batter out are: _____, _____, _____.

6. A regulation softball game consists of _____ innings.

7. Pitching must be done with an _____ motion.

8. A runner is _____ if, after touching the base, overruns it and is returning to it.

9. List three ways softball differs from baseball.

_____   _____

_____

Opinion Poll

Name _____

GOLF

Complete these statements.

1. Always stand _____ and to the _____ of a player about to hit the ball.

2. During play, the player whose ball is _____ from the hole plays first.

3. The player who has the _____ score on a hole plays _____ off the next tee.

4. You must play the ball as it _____. You may not _____ your lie.

5. A loose impediment is a _____ thing and may not be moved. An example is _____.

6. You may move an _____, which is an _____ object.

7. You should _____ ball marks on the green.

8. If your ball is lost out-of-bounds, you must add _____ and play another ball from where you played your last shot.

9. A player has _____ the ball when the stance is taken and the club has been _____.

10. A player may not _____ the club in a hazard.

© 2000 by Parker Publishing Company

Opinion Poll

ANSWER KEY

Fitness

1. 20 minutes, 3 to 5 days
2. 60% to 80%
3. with oxygen
4. oxygen, carbohydrates
5. heavy, few
6. light, many
7. how long, how often, how hard

Soccer

1. 11
2. head, chest, leg (thigh), feet
3. The ball is played from a stationary position; all players must be on their own half of the field; player taking the kick-off must not kick it again until it has been touched by another player.
4. tripping, holding opponent, playing the ball with arm or hand
5. dangerous play, charging when the ball is not close, intentionally obstructing opponent
6. 10
7. the ball has been touched by another player.

Volleyball

1. keep it from hitting the group
2. above the waist
3. back
4. 3
5. a, b, c: foul—team loses service or point
6. 15
7. Play continues until a team is ahead by 2 points.
8. 1 hit
9. server's
   a. right
   b. left

Badminton

1. serving team
2. 15 or 21
3. below
4. right
5. shuttle is hit above the waist or is not in the correct court; head of the racket is not below the hand holding the racket
6. moves before the shuttle is hit
7. player is hit by shuttle, player touches the net, shuttle goes outside the court

Opinion Poll

ANSWER KEY

Pickleball

1. one foot, back
2. underhand, below
3. air, bounce
4. behind
5. diagonally, nonvolley zone
6. 11, 2
7. bounce, bounce
8. out-of-bounds, ball does not clear the net, stepping into nonvolley zone and volleying

Golf

1. still, side
2. farther
3. lowest, first
4. lies, improve
5. natural, leaves or twigs
6. obstruction, artificial
7. repair
8. 1 stroke
9. addressed, grounded
10. ground

Softball

1. smaller
2. pitcher, catcher, 1st base, 2nd base, 3rd base, short-stop
3. left, right, center, and short fielder
4. 9
5. strike out, ground out, fly out
6. 7
7. underhand
8. safe
9. smaller field, underhand pitch, fewer innings

ACTIVITY: SKILL AND FITNESS JOURNALS

Focus/ Knowledge Skill	Equipment Needed	Suggested Grade Levels
To provide students with an opportunity to self-assess ability related to practiced skills. Teachers can also make use of journals in determining skill levels and abilities.	Journal sheet for each student Pencils for each student File folders for each student	Grades 5–8 Modifications for grade levels: Skill and activities listed on journal sheets should be modified for specific classes and grade levels.

Success Notes Provide recognition and/or awards for students who show improvement. This activity can also be used in conjunction with goal-setting activities. Remind students that they all have abilities in various activities, and that if they are "low" in one area they may be "high" in another. When designing journal challenges, build in some activities that require less skill, or a fitness activity allowing all students to experience some success.

MAKING IT WORK

Having students complete individual journals not only provides an opportunity for them to take part in self-assessment but also allows for improvement and recognition of their best attempt. For best success, try the following these steps.

1. Teach, and have students participate in, directed practice before using journals.
2. Have students attempt one to three challenges each time the journals are used.
3. Allow students to repeat a minimum of four trials before recording their best score.
4. A student's best score can be taken from previous attempts or a final attempt.
5. If a student falls below a minimum standard in any item, give that student additional instruction designed to improve skill levels.
6. Students should be asked to analyze their journals, evaluate skills, design a plan for improvement where indicated, and discuss how their skills are best used.

PERSONAL FLOOR HOCKEY JOURNAL
for

_____

Name

How many can you do in one minute?

Challenge	Trials	Best Score
Dribble the puck through 4 cones 3 feet apart		
Pass accurately to a partner 15 feet away		
Receive a pass from a partner 15 feet away		
Shots made from 15 feet		
As a goalie, blocked shots taken from 15 feet away		
Standing with feet apart, move puck around and through your legs		

Fitness Challenge:

Number of jump rope turns _____

Number of push-ups _____

PERSONAL SOCCER JOURNAL for

_____

Name

How many can you do in one minute?

Challenge	Trials	Best Score
Pass a ball to a wall target 15 feet away		
Zigzag dribble between 4 cones 4 feet apart		
Use an overhead throw-in and hit a target on the wall 15 feet away		
Dribble to a cone 30 feet away and back		
Toss a ball in the air and head it		
Punt a ball 30 yards so that it passes between 2 cones 6 feet apart		
Dribble 15 feet, trap it, and immediately turn around and repeat in the other direction		
Drop the ball onto your knee, catch it and repeat		
Defend the goal from a partner's free kick from 20 feet away		

Fitness Challenge:

Number of "figure 8" weaves through cones in 30 seconds		
Number of bench step-ups in 30 seconds		

PERSONAL BASKETBALL JOURNAL
for

_____

Name

How many can you do in one minute?

Challenge	Trials	Best Score
Dribbling through a series of cones		
Cross-over dribble while stationary		
Dribble 10 feet, pivot, dribble back		
Pass a ball around your body		
Figure 8 rotation between legs		
Bounce between legs, catch in back		
Bounce between legs, catch in front		
Chest pass to target 10 feet away		
Bounce pass to target 10 feet away		
Shots made from close range		
Right side/left side lay-ins		

Fitness Challenge:

Number of jump rope turns in 1 minute	
Number of laps around the gym in 2 minutes	

© 2000 by Parker Publishing Company

PERSONAL SOFTBALL JOURNAL
for

_____

Name

How many can you do in one minute?

Challenge	*Trials*	*Best Score*
Pitch underhand and hit a 24″ × 24″ target 30 feet away		
Catch a tossed grounder and immediately throw back to a partner 40 feet away		
Hit a self-tossed ball into "fair" territory		
Toss a ball into the air and catch it with your nondominant hand		
Toss a ball straight up, sit down and catch it		
Do the shuttle run between 2 bases		
With a ball placed between your feet, kick it up and catch it		
Bunt pitcher tossed balls back to the pitcher		

FITNESS CHALLENGE:

Regular push-ups

PERSONAL RACKET SPORTS JOURNAL
for

_____

Name

How many can you do in one minute?

Challenge	Trials	Best Score
Standing in a hula hoop, hit a ball into the air no higher than your head.		
Standing in a hula hoop, hit a ball on the ground.		
Using a forehand stroke, hit the ball into a 24″ × 24″ target 20 feet away.		
Play a ball off the wall from 15 feet away.		
Serve the ball into the opposite court.		
Place hula hoops in various locations in each service court. Drop and hit balls into the hoops.		
Walk from the service line to the net while hitting the ball into the air.		
Alternate forehand and backhand hits off a wall 15 feet away.		

Fitness Challenge:

Number of push-ups completed in 1 minute _____

Number of curl-ups completed in 2 minutes _____

© 2000 by Parker Publishing Company

PERSONAL VOLLEYBALL JOURNAL
for

_____

Name

How many can you do in one minute?

Challenge	Trials	Best Score
Bump a ball against the wall, above the 8-foot line, from 5 feet away.		
Set or bump a ball into the air, make a 90-degree turn, and bump or set again.		
Serve the ball into the receiving court using: underhand serve overhand serve		
Self-toss the ball up and spike it over the net into the receiving court.		
Standing at the net, block a ball tossed by a partner.		
Set the ball against the wall, above the 8-foot line from 5 feet away.		
Bounce the ball on the floor, set it, let it bounce, and dig or set it again.		

Did you use a:

Trainer_____ Volleyball _____ Beachball _____

Fitness Challenge:

Number of jump rope turns in 2 minutes _____

Number of bench steps in 1 minute _____

SECTION 7

Activity Motivators

KEY TO SUCCESS

- **F**ocus is placed on individual students.

- **A**ll students are actively engaged and successful each day.

- **P**rovide developmentally appropriate challenges and activities.

- **S**mile and have fun with each student each day.

Action Motivators

✔ **Pursuing Fitness**
 ➤ Sample Fitness Calendar
 ➤ Student Test Card
 ➤ Goal Setting—Personal Goals
 ➤ Class Records and Goals (Fitness)
 ➤ Class Records and Goals (Skills)

✔ **Physical Education Challenges**
 ➤ District Fitness Challenge
 ➤ District Physical Education Challenge
 ➤ Awards

✔ **Individualizing Learning**
 ➤ Contract Goal Setting
 ➤ Establishing Individualized Programs
 ➤ Active Inclusion for All Students
 ➤ Rewarding Students for Achievement

PURSUING FITNESS:

Traditional fitness monitoring or testing has taken place once or twice each year, with the results used to demonstrate the benefits of the program or to grade student performance. In the attempt to motivate students toward a lifetime of physical activity and fitness, a program that includes daily goal setting, fitness activities, and monitoring works well.

Design class periods to include time for each student to work on a targeted area of physical fitness as noted on the class calendar. This time could be 5 to 10 minutes at the beginning or end of each lesson or during fitness breaks. During this time, students, either individually or in groups, work on a specific targeted area. Once or twice a month, they are given an opportunity to test their achievement by taking a portion of the selected fitness test. They can record the results on a chart like the "Monthly Emphasis Chart" shown here. This process continues throughout the year, giving students numerous opportunities to test. At the end of the year, the best score is recorded as the student's maximum achievement during the year.

SAMPLE FITNESS CALENDAR

Month	Targeted Areas	Test
September	Abdominal Strength and Endurance	Crunches
	Nutrition	Journals
October	Upper Body Strength	Push-Ups
November	Flexibility	Back-Saver Sit & Reach
December	Abdominal Strength Upper Body Strength	Crunches Push-Ups
January	Cardiovascular Endurance Flexibility	PACER* Sit & Reach
February	Cardiovascular Endurance Upper Body Strength	PACER* Push-Ups
March	Abdominal Strength Cardiovascular Endurance	Crunches PACER
April	Upper Body Strength Abdominal Strength	Push-Ups Crunches
May	Cardiovascular Endurance Upper Body Strength	PACER Push-Ups

*PACER = Fitnessgram Assessment of Aerobic Capacity (American Alliance for HPERD and Cooper Institute of Aerobic Research)

Monthly Emphasis Chart

Month: (December)

Emphasis: Abdominal Strength
          Upper Body Strength

Record:

trial date	(crunches)	(push-ups)	Comments
Best Trial			

© 2000 by Parker Publishing Company

Sample Student Test Card

Each time a student takes the test, the date and the score are recorded on the test card. At the end of the year, students review their scores and circle their best attempt. Write the actual student score in the rectangle within the appropriate range.

PACER:
Aerobic Capacity

Needs Improvement	(32) Healthy Range
29	68

Push-Up:
(Upper body strength and endurance)

Needs Improvement	Healthy Range
10	20

Curl-Up
(Abdominal strength and endurance)

Needs Improvement	Healthy Range
18	36

Trunk Lift:
(Low back flexibility)

Needs Improvement	Healthy Range
9	12″

Flexibility:
(Length of hamstring)

Needs Improvement	Healthy Range
8	

Body Composition
(Percentage of body fat)
Based on Body Mass Index Formula

Needs Improvement	Healthy Range	Needs Improvement
22	16.0	

Height_____
Weight_____

Student_____ Age____
School_____ Date____

283

Goal Setting

Personal Goals

Activity	Base Score	Goal
Aerobic Capacity:		
PACER		
Speed Skip		
Flexibility:		
Back-Saver Sit and Reach		
Abdominal Strength:		
Crunches		
Leg-Up Crunch		
Upper Body Strength		
Push-Ups		
Pull-Ups		

In order to reach these goals by _____ (date), I will participate in the following activities with the recommended frequency as outlined by my teacher.

Aerobic Endurance	
Diet	
Flexibility	
Abdominal Strength/Endurance	
Upper Body Strenth/Endurance	

This agreement is made with my full cooperation in trying to achieve my fitness goals.

284 _____ _____ _____
(student signature) (teacher signature) (date)

Class Records and Goals— Fitness

Teacher: _____

Grade: _____

Date: _____

Student Name	Aerobic Endurance		Flexibility	Strength & Endurance	
	Speed Skip	PACER	Sit & Reach	Curl-Ups	Push-Ups
Class Goal/ Class Achievement					

Class Records and Goals— Skills

Teacher: _____
Grade: _____
Date: _____

One Minute	Line Drill		Chest Pass		Crab Walk		Target Throw		Jump Rope		Curl-Ups		Push-Ups		Standing Long Jump	
Student Name	Goal	Ach.	Goal	Ach.	Goal	Ach.	Goal	Ach.	Goal	Ach.	Goal	Ach.	Goal	Ach.	Goal	Ach.
Class Goal/ Class Achievement																

PHYSICAL EDUCATION CHALLENGES

District challenges can be great fun for your students, and at the same time, they further promote your physical fitness and skills focus for all students. You can use one or more of the reproducible "Award" certificates found in this section to enhance student's enjoyment of their participation.

DISTRICT FITNESS CHALLENGE

This challenge activity not only assists students and staff in setting goals but also promotes physical education programs in the district through friendly competition. This challenge is a four-part activity:

Part 1:   Push-ups   **Part 2:**   Curl-ups
          Pull-ups

Part 3:   Back-saver sit and reach   **Part 4:**   PACER (Number
          (Add total inches each   laps run)
          student reaches)

For each activity, a predetermined goal is set for each participating school; for example, the number of students multiplied by 40. After the goal has been established, students at the various schools take a portion of one class period and participate in the event. When all students have completed the activity, total scores are added, divided by the number of participating students, and recorded by both total score and average per student.

Example

The goal for each school is determined by setting an appropriate number of repetitions and multiplying it by the enrollment. All students then perform the activity and record their score. Scores are totaled and compared to the goal. A school average per student can also be posted.

Jefferson   Goal—Total number 22,000—Average per student 40
Middle School   Students enrolled—550
                Number of curl-ups—24,817
                Average per student—43.5

Mason   Goal—Total number 17,880—Average per student 40
Middle School   Students enrolled—447
                Number of curl-ups—17,836
                Average per student—39.9

At the conclusion of each part, participation awards are given to all students who contributed to the total school score. After all four parts have been completed, school awards are given in the following categories:

1. Achieving Your Goal in All Four Activities

2. Highest Total Score (total number of curl-ups, push-ups, inches reached, and PACER laps.)

DISTRICT PHYSICAL EDUCATION CHALLENGE

Each spring, give students from all intermediate and middle-level schools an opportunity to compete, establish personal goals, and set district records in various activities presented during the school year.

Prior to coming together for the one-day district competition, students compete at their individual schools to begin establishing personal goals and setting school records. The top students in each activity then participate in the district Physical Education Challenge Day.

SAMPLE ACTIVITIES

Accuracy Throw: Students throw at a target 40 feet away. Each student has three attempts, using a tennis ball. The target has a center square of 16″ × 16″ and an outer square of 20″ × 20″. Award 3 points for hitting the center square and 1 point for the outer square, and record the total number of points. In the case of a tie, have students make two additional attempts until the tie is broken.

Volleyball Accuracy Set: Students, standing 5 feet from the net, set a self-tossed ball over a 6-foot net into a 2′ × 2′ target placed 10 feet away from the net. Each student is given ten attempts, with the number landing in the target recorded. In the case of a tie, the target is moved back 5 feet, and students are given another five sets.

Juggling: Students may juggle scarves, cubes, clubs, balls, or other juggling equipment you may have. They have 45 seconds to perform a routine to be judged on difficulty, skill, originality, and presentation. Students may also use other apparatus such as balance discs, balance boards, or unicycles to enhance the originality and presentation of their routines.

Speed Rope Skipping: Students jump for 30 seconds. The score is determined by the number of times the rope successfully goes under the feet—1 point for each successful jump. In the case of a tie, a 45-second "jump-off" is held.

Push-Ups: Students perform push-ups to a 3-seconds cadence. Arms must be bent to a 90-degree angle when in the down position, and students must keep with the cadence. Score 1 point for each successful push-up—no maximum. A student may be given two warnings for not bending the arms to 90 degrees or not staying with the cadence. An attempt is over when the student goes off cadence or fails to bend the arms a total of three times.

Pickleball: Use a doubles format. Scoring is to 10 points, with only the serving team able to score a point. Use single elimination format (when a match is lost, the team is eliminated from further play).

Obstacle Course: Students compete in teams of four. Times are recorded and awards given both to individuals and to teams. Add individual times to determine a team score. Each team member is given one attempt to run the course. If a student fails to clear an object or makes a mistake, a 1-second penalty per mistake is assessed. In the case of a tie, an additional attempt is given.

Example
Start—Hop Scotch Hoop Jump—Poly Spot Jump—Hurdles—Under 26″ Bar—Cone Zigzag—Sprint—Finish
(Total distance approximately 80 feet.)

SCHOOL TEAMS
Participants per event, per school:

Pickleball Doubles   Maximum of three teams per school

Obstacle Course   Maximum of four teams per school (two boys,
                                   two girls per team)

All Other Events   Eight students per school

AWARDS
Ribbons can be given up to eighth place, with "Participant" ribbons given to all students.

A "School Spirit" plaque can be given to the school showing the most school spirit, being cooperative and respectful of others, and following directions. You may also want to use one or more of the reproducible awards offered here.

Way to Go!

has successfully completed the

Volleyball Unit

as a

Super Spiker!

_____ _____
Date   Instructor

_____
Principal

Middle School

_____

recognizes

_____

for successfully achieving
personal fitness goals

_____   _____
Teacher   Date

_____
Principal

Awarded To

A Member of

Physical Fitness Team

_____ Date

_____ Instructor

_____ Principal

is presented this

Award of Merit

for outstanding achievement
and successful completion of the

Recreational Sports Program

Teacher

Date

Principal

© 2000 by Parker Publishing Company

293

INDIVIDUALIZING LEARNING

CONTRACT GOAL SETTING

Not all students learn at the same rate, in the same manner, or through the same activities. In accepting this fact, student-centered physical education programs must look to the development of individual student contracts. These contracts are designed to facilitate the development and implementation of personal health and physical activity plans. While skills are taught and practiced in class, students who participate in the Contract Learning Program are expected to monitor their activity patterns outside of class. Through this process, not only are they receiving instruction during class but they are implementing a program of health and positive physical activity outside of the school environment.

To teach and implement this program, makes use of the goal-setting process and activities presented in Section 5.

ESTABLISHING INDIVIDUALIZED PROGRAMS

Program Goals

1. Assisting students in the development, implementation, and monitoring of personal health and physical activity goals.

   a. Establishment of baseline data on physical activity patterns

   b. Establishment of baseline data on health-related fitness levels

   c. Exploration of physical activities that meet personal needs

   d. Exploration of health-related fitness activities that meet personal needs

   e. Development of an action plan designed for participation in specific activities

   f. Monitoring and recording data

   g. Making revisions in plan based on progress and changing needs

2. Providing ongoing support to students in achieving their goals

   a. Development of formal and informal "plan review" sessions

   b. Development of a system of personal rewards for "sticking with" the process

   c. Development of a support system or group within the class—linking students with similar goals and activity patterns so that they may work together and support one another

STUDENT ACTIVITIES

The selection of appropriate student activities must involve a review of all baseline data collected by the student; that is, activity patterns, fitness level, nutritional habits, likes and dislikes, time available, accessibility to equipment and facilities.

Once this review is complete, the Contract Learning Work Sheet is completed.

After completing the Work Sheet, each student schedules a review meeting with the teacher to discuss her or his goals and how they might be achieved. Following the meeting, students begin the development of the actual Contract Learning Plan.

Once students experience success in achieving short-term contract goals, they should expand to goals that will take longer, and more effort, to achieve. Through providing realistic life experiences, in which the student accepts responsibility for learning and achieving, students will begin to develop a sense of commitment. This commitment will lead toward the implementation of a lifelong plan designed to achieve and maintain a healthy and physically active lifestyle.

CONTRACT LEARNING WORK SHEET

For

_____

Short-Term Goal:

_____
_____

Reaching this goal will help me:

_____
_____

Actions I can take to help reach my goal are:

_____
_____
_____

These things could prevent me from reaching my goal:

_____
_____
_____

I can overcome the items listed above by:

_____
_____
_____

These people will support me in achieving my goal:

_____
_____
_____

CONTRACT LEARNING PLAN

For

_____

Today's Date: _____

Target Achievement Date: _____

Actual Achievement Date: _____

Specific Goal Statement (Measurable, Realistic, Attainable):

_____

_____

Specific Action Steps (Activities, Times, Locations):

1. _____

2. _____

3. _____

Monitoring/Review Process (Dates, Actions):

_____

_____

_____

Personal Statements in Support of Achieving This Goal:

_____

_____

_____

Support System:

By signing below, we pledge to support and assist you in the

achievement of your goals.

Name: _____ Signature: _____

Name: _____ Signature: _____

Name: _____ Signature: _____

* *

Signed: _____ *Accepted*: _____

ACTIVE INCLUSION FOR ALL STUDENTS

In all areas of physical education, students with varying levels of ability can be actively involved and successful. These students may be involved in specific units of instruction, assisted by an aide, or fully integrated into the class. In terms of successfully including these students, various strategies may be used. These strategies include:

1. Modification of Instructional Techniques
2. Modification of the Learning Environment
3. Modification of the Activity

Modification of Instructional Techniques
Techniques used to successfully modify instructional techniques include:

1. Modify instructional language—simplify words, limit the number of instructions given at one time, give the instruction followed by a demonstration, repeat instructions and ask students to repeat the instruction.
2. Use concrete examples; select the most appropriate words to convey the meaning; for example, instead of "Make a circle," say, "Join hands to make a circle."
3. Sequence tasks: provide instruction in a sequential manner, giving one task at a time and building to the next.
4. Allow for practice time; provide more practice time and practice formats that implement a buddy system—having students with special needs work with a buddy to provide assistance and reinforcement in the accomplishment of a specific task.
5. Use multisensory techniques—auditory/visual, auditory/tactile, visual/kinesthetic.

Modification of the Learning Environment
Modifications in the learning environment may take the following form:

1. Facility modification—devising temporary ramps, constructing movable or adjustable goals or nets, using bright-colored tape for boundaries.
2. Creating individual spaces—using hula hoops, carpet squares, or poly-spots to define space for each student. A space that is too large, or too small, may be distracting or threatening to some students.
3. Eliminating distractions; possible distractions include extraneous sounds, objects in close proximity to students, large numbers of objects, fast-moving objects, or certain colors.

Modification of the Activity
All physical activities can be modified—with the successful participation of all students in mind. Modifications may include:

1. Placement of students; for example, students with limited mobility can be placed in less active positions, or students with a sensory impairment can be placed close to the teacher or buddy.

2. Length of participation—not all students need, or are able, to participate for the same length of time. Rest intervals can be built in, along with varying the pace of the activity.

3. Changing the skill involved—change motor skills to fit the limitations of specific students; for example, kick with a crutch or catch the ball after one bounce in volleyball.

4. Changing equipment—use brightly colored objects for the visually impaired, use longer or shorter striking implements, lower targets, or use lightweight objects, such as balloons instead of balls.

5. Changing rules—modifying rules to allow for a greater chance of success for all students is acceptable. However, modifications of the rules should not change the focus of the activity.

Including students with disabilities can, and should be, fun and challenging. To be successful and to make the program meaningful, you must be aware of and under individual abilities and limitations.

REWARDING STUDENTS FOR ACHIEVEMENT

Motivation is an important component of any physical activity program. Many factors, both positive and negative, influence student motivation. Negative factors include poor past performance or physical limitations, such as poor coordination, being overweight, or lack of skill. Positive factors include good performance during past activities, having good coordination and skill, and being physically fit.

Traditional programs have rewarded students for achievement—particularly at high levels. Student-centered programs provide rewards and recognition for participation in regular physical activity. The principles of this system focus on the objective of the program—*helping students to develop healthy and physically active lifestyles*. Therefore, activities are organized and rewards provided to students for regular participation, for effort and progress made toward achieving stated goals, and for maintaining a positive attitude toward physical activity.

Selected Resources

Adrian, Gary, Zeke Martin, and Judy Wilson. *87 Alternative Games and Warm-Ups*. Redmond, WA: Bestline Co., 1997.

Carpenter, Jeff, and Diane Tunnell. *Elementary P.E. Teacher's Survival Guide*. West Nyack, NY: Parker Publishing Company, 1994.

Design Group. *Rules of the Game*. New York, NY: Paddington Press Ltd., 1976.

Poppen, Jerry. *Fitness Zone Ahead*. Puyallup, WA: Action Productions, 1996.

Poppen, Jerry. *The BEST of Games That Come Alive!* Puyallup, WA: Action Productions, 1990.

Turner, Lowell, and Susan Turner. *P.E. Teacher's Skill-by-Skill Activities Program*. West Nyack, NY: Parker Publishing Company, 1989.